ACROSS FROM
THE ALLEY
NEXTDOOR
TO THE
POOL ROOM

ACROSS FROM THE ALLEY NEXT DOOR TO THE POOL ROOM

by

Janice L. Booker

REGENT PRESS
Berkeley, California

ISBN 13: 978-1-58790-216-1
ISBN 10: 1-587890-216-8
Library of Congress ControlNumber: 2011921168

First Edition

*Cover photo of 7th and Snyder, circa 1949,
from archives of the Philadelphia History Museum
of the Atwater Kent.*

Manufactured in the U.S.A.
REGENT PRESS
Berkeley, California
www.regentpress.net

Acknowledgments

While this book was in progress, I asked several old friends who had lived in South Philadelphia and had similar experiences to reinforce my memories. Our conversations generated their own recollections of time and place, and we spent warm nostalgic hours reminiscing and reminding each other.

Some who read the finished manuscript were also part of that never forgotten time. For their corroboration of memory and encouragement to have it recorded I thank my cousin and friend, Lorna Shapiro. Frances Miller and Phyllis Steingard were among that group. Naomi Wolfman read the manuscript and was encouraging and insightful along the way. Myrna Weingarten shared similarities that were part of her New York childhood. I checked with Frances Spak and Henry Weinberg for accuracy in mentioning their families.

Although their childhood was completely different, Ellen and Harold Stern read my manuscript and shared their memoirs of a childhood in Nazi Germany with me. For her professional insight and reading with a third eye I thank my colleague and friend, Diana Cavallo, who matched her Italian South Philadelphia neighborhood with many stories which duplicated mine. Sidney Shapiro, of blessed memory, was my source for accuracy in transliteration of Yiddish phrases.

As always, I appreciate the patience and enthusiastic support of my husband, Al, throughout a lifetime of writing projects, and my children, Susan and Ellis, for the joy they have brought me.

Janice L. Booker
November, 2010

THIS BOOK IS DEDICATED TO THE MEMORY OF THOSE
WHO SHARED THESE YEARS WITH ME
My parents, Max and Betty Lekoff and
My brother, Bernie Lekoff

AND TO THE NEXT GENERATION, MY GRANDCHILDREN
Sam and George Booker and
Truman and Ivy Shevick

Table of Contents

CHAPTER ONE

The Streets of South Philly

"Don't you remember me," she asked, hands on hips, curly red hair confined, with difficulty, in a colorful kerchief. "I lived across from the alley next door to the pool room."

My husband and I were having dinner in a neighborhood restaurant. The waitress was brash and likable; an "in your face" endearing intruder, difficult to ignore yet not unpleasantly talkative. Her specific description prompted a vision of the street, although I did not recognize her.

It was the first street I remembered as a child: small row houses in a narrow South Philadelphia street, playmates always available for street games, mothers always in the background talking, shopping, chastising, but ever present. These were the days preceding World War 11 and life in South Philadelphia seemed less complicated than at other times in other places. Street vendors hawked their wares, children's voices dominated the air, families sat on stone steps in the middle of hot summer nights when no one could sleep.

The children played in the streets with imagination their counselor and invented games their guides. Parents were present, visible and in charge. Teachers were venerated and school an awesome responsibility.

Narrow streets, people walking, women talking, children playing, an absence of autos and a high pitch of conversation characterized the neighborhood. Houses were small, typically six rooms and one bathroom squeezed into two stories. The basement, always damp and smelling of mildew, was accessed by a set of narrow stairs leading from the kitchen. These "cellars," as they were called, were never destined to become recreation rooms, or family rooms, or dens. They housed the coal heater, the coal bin, the baskets for collecting the ashes and whatever tools were required to bank the furnace at night and provoke it to action in the morning. The introduction of oil heat was a major convenience, except when winter storms prevented the delivery truck from arriving before the oil ran out. Gas heat was in the future.

I was always afraid to descend those cellar steps. Forgotten nightmares surfaced as I neared the bottom of the stairs, assailed by the dankness and darkness. I was sent to retrieve some root vegetables — potatoes or onions or carrots — which seemed to last much longer in that environment than they do in my hi-tech refrigerator today.

Each house was attached to the house on either side by thin walls of friendship or enmity, depending on each family's definition of "neighborliness." Those were our row houses, a historical signpost of South Philadelphia and emblematic of many Philadelphia neighborhoods. We didn't really know about single homes, and the twin houses that sprung up in the northeast section of the city were a war away. We also didn't know that downtown Philadelphia would become a mecca for row houses with the name "town houses." That future sign of elegant center city housing might have altered the course of our South Philly pride.

In all the houses, one small bathroom on the second floor accommodated families of all sizes. Stall showers or even wall showers in the bathtub were not an option. Most families who liked the idea of a shower bought a hose that attached to the tub faucet with a shower head at the other end. Primitive, but it worked. Actually, that wasn't too different from the European showers of today which detach from a wall unit for hand showering.

I grew up, as did many of my friends, behind a store. My father was a barber and his business was at the corner of Mildred and Shunk streets, a small street between Eighth and Ninth. Living behind the shop had advantages and disadvantages. We lost living space because the store took up so much space. Behind the store was a large kitchen, the center of all household activity, and a small living room. A side door led from Shunk Street into our living room and faced the stairs which led to the second floor where three bedrooms and a bath all opened on a hallway, railroad flat style. The advantage of a corner location was a small edge of privacy as we had only one house on the side and no front porch where neighbors gathered and called to each other across the street or to the house next door.

The entrance to the store was at the corner and the side entrance brought us into our house. The kitchen opened into the barber shop through a doorway. When my father ate lunch or dinner, the door to the shop was always ajar, anticipating the arrival of a customer. That meant my father left the table to take care of business, returning to his meal after the haircut or shave. I was always angry that his meals were disrupted, especially at dinner when the whole family was together. My parents seemed to accept those interruptions as part of doing business. I'm sure our family was not unique. Every customer took precedence so that throughout the neighborhood scores of South Philadelphia meals were disturbed when the store door opened.

Privacy was a luxury enjoyed only in single homes in

Wynnefield or the unknown and mysterious suburbs, where houses were separated by greenery. The only green in South Philadelphia was the watermelon rind on the wagon of the fruit huckster or the occasional lime water ice from the cart that was paraded on the streets on hot summer days.

Next door to our house on the Eighth Street side was a gas station, a constant source of irritation to my mother who said she could smell the gas fumes even in her sleep and insisted our sheets and towels, hung out to dry on twine clotheslines in the back yard facing the station, were discolored and smelled of gas and oil. The station was called "Jaffe's Flying A," named after the owner and the gasoline brand. Mr. Jaffe had placed a small bench in an outdoor niche underneath his kitchen windows where customers could wait while their cars were being serviced. This bench became an oasis for my cousin and me on sultry summer nights. We were teenagers together and clung to each other during times of family stress. We would meet at Jaffe's bench on summer nights about 10 p.m. and talk for hours. We were not afraid; we were never accosted, there was little traffic passing on the street and we could talk our teenage hearts out until our eyelids betrayed the time. At 10 P.M. we'd call each other and say "Meet you at Jaffe's bench." And there we would sit, for hours, often until after midnight, talking, talking, talking. From schoolwork to professional ambition, from boys to politics, from family matters to lipstick, no subject was taboo. Subjects ranged from crushes to our joint awakening interest in left-wing politics. We explored our futures, exchanged philosophies, wondered about our lives, and experienced the deep confidence that only teenage girls can exchange.

We talked and talked. Those nights are still sacred in my memory. Our joy in each other was that no adult could share these confidences and questions. We were alone in the world and felt a kindred spirit we often still share.

We were comfortable sitting on a street corner at that hour.

Auto traffic was minimal, people passing by were virtually non-existent, and we had no experience with neighborhood fears. We were surrounded by the quiet slumber of the neighborhood and occasional night noises, for it was summer and windows were open. Sated with conversation, often about 1 a.m., we walked the short distance to our homes, again without fear, until the next night at Jaffe's bench.

The streets were not quiet during the day. Vendors, solicitors, visitors, and family members traveled the streets. Once a year a man with a paint brush and a can of white paint toured the neighborhood, stenciling each home address on the curb. After the deed was done, he asked the homeowner for 25 cents. This was usually given without complaint.

Strangers were not unwelcome but rarely appeared. An unrecognizable visitor, especially a man wearing a suit, was considered a collector of past due bills and his presence created a wariness on the part of neighbors.

The street was a busy place in good weather, a sort of counterpart of an old world town market. First, horse-led wagons and then trucks carried anything from seltzer to dry goods; in fact, for those housewives who limited their corner store shopping, many home and food necessities could be purchased by listening for the hawking sounds of the delivery men and the clop-clop of their shops on wheels.

The street merchants seemed never to change, the products trumpeted by the same person, year after year. Somehow the shouts of "Good, sweet watermelon," or "Get your ice now," or even, "Fresh eggs from the farm" sounded quite natural and normal. But there was something in the voice of the Javelle water man that sounded eerie as his cadence rang out in the street, "Jaavelllle water," a kind of strung out song that rose to a screeching high in the middle, with the last syllable swallowed in the depths of his throat. Sometimes, a mother was occupied the moment she heard the familiar sound, perhaps with a younger child, or hands in sudsy water, or, for more affluent families, on the telephone. Then, the older child was told: "Tell the Javelle man to wait. I'll be right there. Hurry!"

Javelle water was a major necessity. My memory is that it was only available from the back of a wagon or truck. This was ordinary bleach, an essential for doing laundry. Clothes were washed at home, of course, by the women of the household, bending over washtubs filled with steaming water and suds. The work was accomplished by back-breaking elbow grease. When the first mechanical washers appeared, the wringers required almost as much work as the washboards. Clothes were often hung out of doors even in winter and frozen stiff, because whatever fresh air clung to the clothes was considered healthy. When the weather was too bad, the cellar substituted and the clotheslines were never taken down. Ironing usually repaired the condition of clothes taken off the line, but for any items not ironed, their harsh texture brought the reminder of winter weather to any part of the body in contact with it. When automatic dryers came into use, we suddenly realized that bath towels were not meant to scrape abrasively against our wet bodies.

My mother, a faithful reader of women's magazines, bought an advertised appliance that substituted for the hand ironing of flat items. She and I spent many nights in the cellar with our new addition called a "mangle." She cheerfully ironed the sheets, towels, and all items that fit over the mechanism by operating a foot peddle, while I sat by her side, reading aloud the articles or short fiction in the current issue of Ladies' Home Journal or Redbook.

The corner grocery store or fruit store was the focus of in-store shopping, as well as the community news center. But with limited refrigeration, home delivery meant fresher foods, so items such as milk, bread, and ordinary often-used products, eggs and cheese and butter, were frequently bought at the point-of-purchase front door from farmers who all seemed to come from New Jersey. Milk and bread, however, came from major companies and were delivered by the driver/salesmen who quickly became neighborhood fixtures. Their personalities, as well as their personal lives, were fodder for as much gossip as a neighbor's wayward son or an errant husband.

"Parkie," our family bread man, seemed old to me because of his silver hair. I didn't see much of it, as it was covered with a cap that matched his neat, brown uniform. His name came naturally; he represented the Parkway Baking Company. Parkie had a dual occupation. In addition to delivering sliced, packaged white bread and occasional boxes of white, powder-covered doughnuts, he was also the neighborhood numbers writer, covering the same territory as his delivery route. In the days before state lotteries and Jersey casinos, the numbers game was the only game in town that gave poor people the hope that luck might shine on them. Instead of millions, they hoped for a win that would give them ten or twenty dollars. That was considered a real windfall. The numbers game held the hope of a financial gift, perhaps enough to finance a weekend in Atlantic City, or a more needy family might even settle for a new living room lamp. Little did these hopeful players know, or possibly care, that their pennies found their way to major crime syndicates.

Parkie collected the numbers slips and the small change that went with them. My knowledge of this investment scheme ends there: I never knew what happened to them after that, but all the kids knew he was the numbers broker. One day a police car appeared on the scene. When Parkie saw this, he panicked, not knowing whether the police were after him or some other petty racketeer. At the time he spotted the car, he happened to be talking to my father, who was shaving a customer. He made eye contact with my father, who nodded imperceptibly, and the next thing I knew the envelope with the numbers slips and cash was placed behind the sliding doors of our new floor console radio and record player. My heart pounded until the police car disappeared. Suppose the police came into the house and found the stash? Would they confiscate our new entertainment center as evidence?

Parkie's deliveries were made in a shiny, clean van, with the name of the bread company in white letters on its side. The color of the truck, chocolate brown, matched Parkie's uniform. His vehicle was the most modern of the street peddlers.

Mr. Minerva, the butter and egg farmer, came in a tacky pickup truck from Atco, New Jersey. At that time, he was the only Italian person I knew, so I considered him highly exotic. One day, he appeared with a young boy, about my age, who, even in my nine year old gender blindness, I knew was extremely handsome. Anthony, or "Ansony" as my little brother called him, became his father's frequent companion and my secret crush for the next few years. On Tuesdays, Mr. Minerva's delivery day, I started questioning my mother about our dairy needs: didn't we need more cheese for a Sunday visit from relatives? Wouldn't it be a good idea to buy more butter? Each additional purchase gave me more time to gaze at Anthony, as I stood next to my mother as she and Mr. Minerva exchanged purchases, money and pleasantries.

Eventually, because of larger and better supplied neighborhood markets, and Mr. Minerva's age, both he and Anthony vanished from our front door. About a decade later, I learned from the newspaper that an Anthony Minerva Jr. had been found dead in his car on a New Jersey country road, clearly the victim of a homicide. Subsequent stories revealed that there was a cheese war between Anthony, attempting to enlarge his father's business, and a major cheese distributor in the area, rumored to be connected with organized crime.

Mr. Minerva's products did not include milk, which was delivered daily, heralded by the early morning rhythmical clatter of horses' hooves on the asphalt street, and the different sound that echoed when the hooves encountered bricks. This was the first sound announcing the new day, making alarm clocks obsolete for early risers. The horse and wagon also became history, as motor vehicles replaced the overworked animals. Milk cartons were in the future. The unhomogenized milk arrived in glass bottles which were placed at the front door. When the temperature was below freezing, the cream, its thickness placing it at the crown of the milk bottle, froze. In this state, the icy white column pushed up the thin cardboard top, creating a convex invitation to scoop up the cream crystals. In our house, the cream was reserved for my mother's coffee and the rest of us, unknowingly, drank healthy, fat-free milk.

Fruit and vegetable hucksters, too, were an important shopping aid. The housewives gathered at the back of the truck, examining the melons, lettuce and plums with the eye of a sharpshooter. Melons got plugged; that is, holes were made in them by the driver/salesman which produced about a square inch of fruit, so that the "missus" could judge for herself the ripeness and tastiness of the product. The ladies, satisfied with their choices, were then in a position to bargain, depending on the prices of the same products at the corner store.

I often wondered what happened to the rejects, each melon now with a perfect hole in its center. I concluded the seller took them all home and his wife and children had a melon-filled summer. Neat supermarket packages, with items encased in plastic wrap, make taste judgements prior to dessert impossible.

Some fruit deserved special vehicles, so that watermelon was transported alone; no competition from other melons. But when the men came around with their trucks, shouting "good, sweet watermelons, cheap" the neighborhood children gathered around as their mothers taste-tested the crunchy red centers. It was unthinkable to buy it without trying it. Chunks of the fruit were distributed as if they were hors d'oeuvre at a cocktail party. The banana man was also a minimalist, offering only his sweet wares at 5 cents a bunch.

Hot corn was available from, who else, the "corn man," who kept a pail of boiling water bubbling on a fire. The golden ears of corn were pulled from the pail with tongs and smeared with butter, which melted down the chin and on the clothing.

Today, walking down the aisles of neighborhood supermarkets, various companies hawk their new products and offer "tastings." A judicious choice of markets could supply a light lunch or afternoon snack. The process is a little better organized and possibly more sanitary than the backs of trucks on the street, but the ultimate goal is the same: sell what you can to consumers' critical palates by offering tidbits.

A lesser taste test occurred when the iceman came. Because many homes in the thirties still used iceboxes for refrigeration, usually tall wooden rectangles with chrome handles, they needed to have ice to keep them functioning, so the iceman was even more essential than the fruit trucks. The truck, or horse and wagon, proceeded on its journey at a crawl, while the driver shouted his wares, in this case, only one. He stopped midway down the street while his potential customers (he could be pretty certain of sales with his necessary, non-competitive product) gathered around to determine how large a block of ice was needed. An ice pick was used to separate the necessary section of ice requested from the larger bulk. That's where the kids came in. As the ice pick did its carving, slivers of ice flew through the air, but not for long. Little hands stretched to receive them, and very few of these minor stalactites hit the ground. I can still taste the burlap that encased the ice to keep it from melting and its taste clung even to the bits of ice as we kids chewed the morsels, appreciating their coldness in the summer heat.

By the '40s, most homes had refrigerators, but why waste the cold temperatures and possible increased electricity costs when cold air was free outside your window? As soon as the first frost made us shiver, environment seemed the natural way to go, without even realizing the benefits of limiting electricity use. At the first hint of winter window boxes appeared, the heavy cord connecting the refrigerator to electricity was yanked, and foods needing cold to be preserved were placed in the window box. Fingers got a little frosty when milk was needed, but the window boxes served well until early spring made its debut.

The horseradish man appeared before holidays, with his beets, vinegars and whatever seasonings made my eyes water and my nose twitch when he grated the beets to produce fresh horseradish. The knife sharpener expert was a fixture, marching down the street with self-assurance, wielding his honed instruments and attracting the women who admired his prowess and needed his skills to practice their own kitchen expertise.

When the streets were not used for marketing, they, and the sidewalks, were the children's playground. We had no swings, sand boxes, jungle gyms or tricycles; nor were there parks with nannies, pre-school programs, Head Start or community centers with nursery rooms. Day care meant you left the baby with a neighbor while you ran down to the corner to buy some forgotten item for dinner. There was only the street and our imagination, and whatever items we could sneak from the house to represent something else.

Stays from our mothers' girdles were important. When scraped quickly over a stone stoop, the result was a quick flash of electricity, a magical blue spark without a match. We competed to see whose spark could last the longest. Competition was a major component of any game. "I win" was a triumphant shout of victory, followed quickly by the reinforcing "You lose!"

We children didn't have much in the way of entertainment that we didn't provide for ourselves. Certain specific activities were standard: jump ropes for girls, stick ball for boys. Scooters were made by fathers from orange crates confiscated on trash day from the corner grocery store, fashioned with more or less complexity atop abandoned skate wheels. They worked just fine. Fruit baskets were essential to play basketball. A stray piece of lumber served as a backboard, a basket with the bottom removed was nailed to it, and voila! Basketball.

The most competitive street game, played only by girls, was hopscotch. I use the more popular name because few people would recognize what we called it: "potsy." I learned as an adult that potsy was the name used for this game in South Philadelphia and certain parts of Brooklyn, a semantic mystery I never tried to unravel. In the first house I remember, on Darien street, there must have been an inventive sidewalk concrete artist, either with a wry sense of humor or an affection for girls, because the sidewalk in front of my house duplicated an exact potsy configuration, otherwise etched on the concrete with chalk. Naturally, my sidewalk (or pavement as we called it) was the center of this play activity.

Roller skates and bicycles completed the equipment that supplemented our imagination. The lack of more tangible playthings was caused not only by limited funds; the absence of technology had a lot to do with dependence on ourselves for play ideas. No video games, no television and no computers made us dependent on movies and radio for passive recreation. Radio was in its heyday; television not even imagined by ordinary people. Our play was based on radio characters or, in many cases, the magical influence of movies. Somehow the unknown future was grist for children's creative minds. We conjured up plots, subplots and solutions so that the hero always won. Batman and Robin and Buck Rogers were our favorite subjects for improvisation. Buck Rogers gave us the opportunity to create our own electronic and mechanical future with ideas yet unknown, perhaps still unknown. Adventures of Batman and Robin, Superman, the Green Hornet and the Shadow were often based on radio plots which fused with our play and what we believed to be improvement on the scripts, for we added characters and situations that we were certain the creators of the serials would use, if only they knew about them.

Although these re-enactments of radio serials were gender blind, other games were not, with a strict separation of what the girls played and the rougher games reserved for boys. Jumping through hoops and making the yo-yo bounce up and down were non-sexist, but rougher games which required some physical power were reserved for the boys. "Buck buck number one is coming" (a game I've heard Bill Cosby talk about in his home town comedy skits) required boys to run and jump on each other's backs, much too athletic for the girls, especially because we wore dresses for play, not pants, and that would have been too unseemly. Jump rope and hi-li were for the girls, but boys also played hi-li and often engaged in weekly competitions at the Broadway Theater. We also did some handiwork, making rag dolls out of old socks or using a gizmo called a "horse rein" to wrap fabric around prongs and pull these strands through a hole in the bottom of the gadget. It emerged as a kind of braid and eventually, given enough summer days with nothing to do, we wound these pigtail like ropes around each other and with patience and time they turned into a kind of oval mat. We called it a "rag rug."

We made cat's cradle out of string wound around our fingers and turned flour and water into paste to cement odd shapes on paper. The girls played house and school; the boys played ball. When we complained to our mothers that we had nothing to do, they told us to hit our heads against the wall. They didn't mean it literally, of course; they were telling us to find our own amusement.

Ice cream trucks bearing popsicles and frozen bananas were in the future, but there was a happy precedent. On summer evenings a man appeared, pushing a cart which housed a large quantity of shaved ice and multiple bottles of syrup, in flavors ranging from deep chocolate to pale vanilla, and every color in-between.

The ice was piled in a paper cup and the sweet syrup, color and flavors of the customer's choice, poured over it. This was called "Italian water ice," so named by either the country of its invention or the ethnicity of the purveyor.

In warm weather, about once a week, just as dusk was draping the street with its shadowy curtain, a figure appeared at the corner, a one-legged, diminutive African-American man, on crutches, singing, a small monkey attached to one crutch with a tattered rope, a tambourine in one outstretched paw. As the man hobbled down the street, his reedy voice quavering on high notes of familiar melodies, the children clustered in awe as the grownups came forth to toss some change into the tambourine. I dreamed about this man for years, filled with curiosity about him, coupled with fear and apprehension. There was something eerie about the tableau which made me uneasy, and I was grateful for those rainy nights when this entertainment was bypassed.

Summer loomed to us kids like an endless horizon, days filled with outdoor play with friends, trips to the library, ice cream cones after dinner, and air-conditioned movies. Home air-conditioning was rare, but watering holes were not. These were the street fire hydrants, at least one per block. We called them "plugs," a South Philadelphia nomenclature I never heard in any other area. Philadelphia's political system featured a network of committeemen — I don't recall any women in this position — whose job it was to represent the particular needs of his constituency to the city government, as well as to grant favors. The local committeeman was keeper of the key to the hydrant. What power! When the temperature reached unbearable heights (he must have had an acceptable number in his head) he was approached by a committee of mothers. Often, he complied; sometimes not. I have no idea on what conditions he based his largesse. When the answer was "yes," out came the key and on came the water. A gush of cold water cascaded down the street and all the kids, and sometimes the grownups, in their street clothes, ran for this aquatic refreshment. The piece de resistance was when someone with a more than adequate butt pushed that part of his or her anatomy up against the mouth of the hydrant and created a shower. Why standing barefoot in the street seemed more sanitary than swimming in a chemically cleansed swimming pool was part of the lore of the neighborhood.

During the summer, neighborhood swimming pools were available. They weren't the elaborate pools of today, replete with play equipment and gardens. They were indoors, fairly small and rank with chlorine, but I remember this from hearsay and not experience. The threat of polio loomed like a specter over our parents' minds, especially in summer and in particular when exposed to other children. There was the added danger of families unknown to the mothers. So neither my friends nor I were ever allowed to even approach the neighborhood pool. And because summer camp was not a possibility financially and day camps not yet on the recreational horizon, I never learned to swim.

Some July and August nights were murderously hot. We moved bedclothes and pillows to the floor, on the theory that cooler air migrated to the lower part of the room. But there was no cool air, on the floor or any other place in those stifling rooms. On such nights the entire family; in fact, the entire neighborhood, went outside and sat on steps and porches, hoping to "catch a breeze." When the committeeman joined the outdoor crowd, he brought along his precious key, and everyone cooled off under the showers of the hydrant in the middle of the night, kids and grownups alike.

Rain created a problem in summer. We looked longingly at the street as the hot asphalt, its composition altered by the rain, sent up clouds of steam into the air. Outdoor games were reserved for summer when the street was the only place to play, although winter weather did not keep us indoors. Snow was welcome; it provided the opportunity to build forts in the street, snow and ice enclosures which we thought of as igloos but called "forts," large enough for several children to sit in. Matches seemed to be more available to kids, so we lit a small fire and roasted potatoes over it, the precedent, I suppose, to backyard barbecues. I don't ever remember potatoes baked in an oven tasting as good.

We didn't know our play was limited by what had not yet been invented. We didn't know there were other children who went away to camp during the summer and rode horses and swam in lakes and pools. Our advantage was we didn't think we were deprived. Our playtime ranged as far as our imagination took us, and we soared through our days always knowing the Lone Ranger and Tonto would triumph only because of our intervention.

There was no supervision of street play. Unspoken rules held forth: the community of universal motherhood was on guard. Every child was every mother's protectorate. Fights were settled by parental intervention, and sometimes unresolved after the mothers carried on the fight among themselves. We didn't have sleep-overs. We also didn't spend a lot of time in each other's houses. The street served as our social arena, and when invited to a girlfriend's house, we had warnings from our mothers. "If her mother asks you any questions about our family, say you don't know." I never knew from what depths those suspicions sprung, but I did know they had to do with money, or the lack of it, which was pretty much everyone's circumstance. We were also not supposed to eat in anyone else's home, because the mother might think our family could not afford a proper meal. That's so different from today, when children are accustomed to "play dates" followed by an invitation to stay for lunch or dinner. Visitations from one household to another were often unannounced. Even those families who boasted a telephone did not call in advance to announce their intention to "come calling." The reason: If you told them you were planning a visit, they might feel obliged to prepare food and you didn't want to obligate them. But if they weren't home when you arrived, there was a little feeling of annoyance. A no-win situation.

The exceptions were relatives. Because in those days relatives generally lived within a few blocks of each other, we could eat at relatives' homes. But that, too, was subject to who was talking to who at any given time. Arguments among family members seemed frequent, and perhaps proximity had something to do with that. It was pointless to have family reunions or special occasion parties, as siblings, aunts, grandparents, and other family members constantly bumped into each other at the corner grocery store or the butcher or the baker, or just crossing the street. Fortunately, reconciliation came as quickly as an argument, frequently associated with a holiday celebration. Yom Kippur was often a perfect makeup time, and outside the synagogue doors, after the shofar blew, the perfect place. Sometimes the good feelings lasted until Passover, when an invitation to Seder further smoothed over ruffled feathers until the next disagreement.

The women in the neighborhood didn't have jobs outside the home. A woman who worked before marriage, or before children, or after children were grown, was said to "go to business," and there was a hushed respect for her. Women of that generation were unqualified for commerce, and the accepted assumption was that a woman's job was to take care of her home and family. And that was plenty of work. Most women did not have household help. Sometimes, before a major holiday, a houseworker came for a day and the housewife worked right alongside her. No nannies, no maids, no dishwashers, few chemical cleaning aids, just hard work. Housecleaning was tedious and many women believed that "eating off the floor" or such unrealistic expectations of their housekeeping was tantamount to their regard as good wives and mothers. The latter included the cleanliness of their children's clothes, the shine on their shoes and cooking to perfection; in short, being a "balaboosta," Yiddish for exemplary housekeeper.

Because finances were everyone's bottom line, it was the job of the homemaker to cut costs by seeking bargains in food and clothing, stretching budgets, managing household accounts, and being generally thrifty. That left little for frivolity in entertainment or clothing. Women preened when their houses were pronounced "spotless." Those with more than two children were considered paragons of domesticity, especially if they were deemed to have an immaculate house. Front steps were scrubbed several times a week, sidewalks swept, and windows washed diligently including second story windows.

I shudder when I think about the women sitting outside the second story windows, on the window sill, frame across their lap to act as a guard against falling. I remember walking along Shunk Street on my way home from Thomas Junior High School and seeing my mother's torso come into view out the window. I was terrified, fearful of shouting hello from the street as my voice might startle her into falling. So I hurried my pace, quietly entering the house on tiptoe and announced myself softy as I walked quickly up the steps to the second floor. I approached her and put my hand on her thigh inside the window, casually, thinking she might not notice my fear, and I stayed that way until all the windows were finished. It never occurred to me to say "Please don't do this; it scares me." All the women did it, sometimes shouting to each other a few windows away. My mother loved opera and often sang arias as she washed the windows.

Change of seasons brought intense housekeeping rituals. Spring cleaning was a major player in the drama. Warm weather meant transforming the house from winter to summer. Rugs, drapes, slipcovers and bed linens all had to be changed to allow for warmer weather. The mohair living room sofa and chairs were now covered with cotton slipcovers. The wool rug was taken out into the back yard, hung over the clothes lines, and beaten with paddles to release the dust that the floor vacuum missed during the winter season. It was then stored in the basement, after being wrapped in brown paper, and replaced with a cotton braided rug. Whatever heavy drapes covered the windows, satin or brocade, were replaced with cotton or the forerunner of Dacron, in a light color, and the dark-hued kitchen and bedroom curtains were replaced with lighter colors and filmier fabrics. The house was then ready for warm weather and just before the High Holidays in the fall, all were replaced with the darker colors and heavier fabrics of winter. This happened every year.

These rituals were reassuring. Life "on the block" became a pattern that gave people a sense of community. Those folks who had emigrated felt secure; they thought they had taken this voyage to make their children's lives better but saw their own lives safer with possibilities they hadn't even considered. People shared their lives in a very public way. The houses were too small, the streets too narrow, the children too noisy for neighbors to be remote. Lives were shared – people fought, laughed and cried together. It was these South Philadelphia streets, primarily a mix of Italian and Jewish families, that spawned the entertainers and professors of the next generation. The child whose mother was called to school periodically to witness his bad behavior became a Pulitzer Prize winner, his neighbor rose to the heights of the entertainment world, and the young woman who sat next to me in study hall has a national reputation as an educator.

Each adult who grew up in South Philadelphia has a story to tell. This is mine.

CHAPTER TWO

Getting Away From It All

Florida was a place on the map, the Caribbean was somewhere else in the world and Europe was where our families came from and didn't want to go back to. Vacations were what rich people took, and a cruise ship evoked the memory of traveling ten days in steerage. For most South Philadelphians, an evening's recreation meant playing cards around somebody's kitchen table, and, after the game, enjoying a glass of tea and home made mandelbrot or strudel. A day trip to Atlantic City was considered a vacation. No family took a week or two to go to the mountains or the seashore. Men who ran a storefront retail business were afraid to lock the doors, lest their customers find another source for their needs. Those folks who ran their own service businesses (tailor, house painter, paperhanger, floor-layer) couldn't afford to lose the income. Any overnight trip was usually to a relative who had a pullout sofa.

But a trip to the seashore, which always meant Atlantic City, created the same kind of excitement two weeks at Las Vegas or Cape Cod might create today. First, one had to find a means of transportation. Most families did not own a car, but if they did, that made the trip more feasible. But there was always the train. The Reading Railroad Station, when it was located at 12th and Market Streets, scheduled daily trains to and from Atlantic City. However, for a cheaper fare, one could board that train in Camden, paying five cents to cross the Delaware River by ferry. Because that saved a few pennies, that was often the route of choice. There was a non-financial price to pay for using the train. These trains burned coal, and the fine dust settled on skin and clothing, making a dip in the ocean a cleansing ritual.

We took the Seventh Street trolley car north to Market Street, and then another ride, via a coupon called a "transfer," free of additional charge, east to the foot of Market Street, then five minutes on the ferry to Camden where we boarded the train to Atlantic City. If we were fortunate enough to hitch a car ride with someone, the trip was less costly and more fun. If two families shared a car ride, the protocols were standard. The guest riders paid for gas and bridge tolls to compensate for the "wear and tear" assaults on the vehicle for the sixty mile trip.

Intense decision-making preceded the outset of the trip. Before the Atlantic City Expressway, the question was: Do we take the White Horse Pike or the Black Horse Pike? Which highway had more stop signs and lights? Which highway had more traffic? Where would we find more gas stations with rest rooms along the way? That decision made, we were on our way, brown bags or shoe boxes filled with rolls, salami, hard boiled eggs, home-made cookies, fruit and a salt shaker. As we approached the seashore, via Absecon and Egg Harbor, my nostrils quivered and my heartbeat increased as I knew we were almost there. The ground next to the highway started to look sandy, with tufts of scrubby grass pushing through the taupe-colored sand. And then there was the smell. I swore I could smell the mingled odors of sand and sea. I anticipated that aroma as the herald of being at the seashore. I later learned I was actually smelling beached dead fish. There was no mistaking we were on our way "down the shore," as Philadelphia jargon would express going to the beach.

We wore our bathing suits under our clothing and carried brown paper bags with special grooming items, such as comb, brush, towels, and lipstick if there were teenagers among us, possibly some candy bars, rapidly melting in the heat. Extras such as cold drinks and frozen custard were purchased on several of the many forays onto the boardwalk. "Walking the boards" was a familiar and constant exercise when in Atlantic City, but the dank and damp underpart was just as familiar. Without a hotel room or a "rich" relative fortunate enough to have a small apartment near the beach, which meant a two block walk, we doffed our clothing under the boardwalk to reveal the bathing suit. That was fine for our arrival, but when departure time came, the bathing suits, often wool, were wet and itchy under our clothing, which quickly darkened as the wetness of the bathing suit followed the natural course of water. But that was a small price to pay for a day at the seashore.

We soaked up the sun, before the days warning of the dangers of excessive sun exposure. Our sun screen was an oily substance whose purpose was to enhance tanning, and which produced a lacquered, glossy finish on our skin, not unlike the patina of furniture polish.

Jumping the waves was accompanied by screeches and shouts. The beach was always crowded, a panoramic multitude of bodies, getting the most out of this day with sun and sand. The sun, dazzling in its enveloping heat, embraced the crowd. The salt spray tickled our faces and the sand sprinkled our food. We didn't care. We children dug trenches in the sand, wondering to each other if we would reach China if we dug deep enough. And as we scanned the horizon, hands creating an awning over our heads, we wondered what country lay beyond the water and what sat at the bottom of the ocean. Did the ocean have a bottom? How long could we stay under water before drowning? If we built a sand castle beyond where the tide couldn't reach it, would it still be there tomorrow even if we weren't?

Sometimes a family scraped together enough savings to spend a week at the seashore. Housing was in a converted old house on Atlantic or Pacific Avenue, once the home of some titan, now converted to a rooming house with ten or twelve bedrooms, a communal kitchen, a large front porch, and an outdoor shower to wash one's feet of sand before going indoors. The accommodations most opted for were called "koch aleins," in Yiddish, literally, "cook alone." The "boarders" had a room which served as bedroom and sitting room for the family, a shared bathroom with other occupants, a partial shelf in the community refrigerator for the food they bought — restaurants were out of the question — and a burner on the oversized kitchen stove to do their cooking. Tables in the eating room were covered with the same oilcloth material that covered the kitchen tables at home, and each family was given an allotment of dishware and utensils for meals. Families shared tables in the kitchen, or, in a house that once was really grand, the dining room.

The wife/mother was responsible for the shopping, the preparation of the meals, the cleanup, and the room in which the family slept. The daily excursions to the beach, often several blocks, included sand chairs, suntan lotion, a packed lunch, towels, and of course, the children. Back and forth each day. Still, it was away from the city and a welcome change of pace.

Beach chairs, colorfully striped canvas stretched over collapsible wooden frames, did double duty. Not only were they part of the paraphernalia loaded to take to the seashore, they were the patio furniture of record on the sidewalks of South Philadelphia on hot summer nights when people couldn't sleep and sat out in the dark, lounging on the beach chairs, hoping the night would cool, talking over the events of the day and the fantasies of the future.

As our time on the beach ended, we "walked the boards." As teenagers, we hoped to accidentally come upon our latest crush, or any member of the opposite sex we knew. Sometimes, approached by some young men we did not know, we returned the flirtation until we sensed it might go further, and then scurried away in a panic.

Water was seductive, and southern New Jersey had a lot of it in the form of lakes. In some places there were cedar lakes, believed to have curative and medicinal properties. I remember going to Almonessen and Browns Mills. Because few families had their own cars, a group was assembled, one of whose members had access to a pickup truck. Several families would pack up the brown paper bags with the requisite hard boiled eggs, salt, rolls, fruit, and cake. More adventurous housewives brought brisket or chicken. Most food was precooked. Potato salad was essential, as were housewives' baked goods specialties. The driver and two others squeezed into the narrow cab and the other passengers sat on benches in the open truck. The destination was one of the many South Jersey lakes which boasted a small beach and public bathrooms where people could change into bathing suits. The townships, welcoming the day visitors because of what they might stop in town to buy, placed picnic tables in shaded groves and some, extending their welcome, included barbecue pits. (My mother would have eschewed these, as the grates would never have been clean enough, holding a history of previous users.) At the end of the day, sunburnt, well-fed and tired, the children usually fell asleep on the way home while the adults talked about the good day. And it was.

My parents tried to duplicate this experience years later when they bought a small vacation house in a lakeside community in

Franklinville, New Jersey. The area was one where many Jewish settlers, years before, had gone into the business of raising and selling chickens. Many of the farms were still there, surrounded by the lush verdant oasis of the lakes. My parents called this their "country home" and were as proud of this as if it were a Newport mansion.

The little community in Franklinville consisted of about a dozen homes, and many of the homeowners were related. The houses skirted a small beach and a lake. The conveniences were minimal, often lacking the ordinary comforts of home which, in the 50s and 60s, would have included washers and dryers, a sprinkling of air-conditioners, and much more space. But it was the country, and it was a second home. A vacation home!

The tiny houses were what we called "bungalows." Each one had a porch almost the size of the house. My parents had an impressive double lot, and my father, who loved grass and trees despite his hay fever, sat proudly on his gas mower, keeping his grass as smooth and green as a golf course. On weekend evenings the men gathered in one house or another to play cards. The pots consisted of pennies; a win of two or three dollars was a windfall. Poker was the game of choice. They sat at a kitchen table, sipping coffee and sharing a plate of the hostess' dessert specialty. The women sat on the porch, chatting. Cards were also a staple of evening entertainment in the city, with stakes the same for games of pinochle or poker. The women didn't play cards, and mah jong was not their style. Conversation was.

Kids also played cards. Our games were War and Fish and Knuckles, and they were played on the outdoor steps, in the house, on the sidewalk and anywhere a deck of cards could be shuffled and distributed. All victors were ecstatic; all losers crestfallen. Competition existed in card games as much as in any board game or street activity.

Teenagers used leisure time quite differently. The boys "hung out," usually in front of a large plate glass window at a corner candy store, drugstore, or luncheonette, watching the girls go by as they swung their key chains from the pockets of their zoot suited pegged pants. The girls walked past the corners, hoping for flirtatious compliments while tossing their hair. On Saturdays we paraded up and down Seventh Street, the major shopping area for the neighborhood where all the action was, with hair in curlers, hoping that would signify we had a date that evening. Often we didn't. Before e-mail, cell phones, and other technological paraphernalia that makes communication instant, the telephone was the lifeline of teenagers. Walking home with a friend from school, leaving her at her front door five minutes from our own, was no reason not to make an immediate phone call to her to continue the conversation.

Names did not yet appear in the phone book saying "children" with a phone number different from that of the parents. For my fifteenth birthday I was thrilled to be presented with my own phone for my room. Not my own number; merely an extension phone. But to me, it signified my family's recognition that I was mature enough to hold telephone conversations in the privacy of my own room. This was power!

Probably the most enjoyable and frequent entertainment was having guests. Dinner parties were reserved for family occasions and holidays, but friends were invited for an evening of cards, conversation and dessert. South Philadelphia row homes had no patio, terrace, deck or lawn, but they did have cement paved backyards. As a very young child, I remember my parents having backyard watermelon parties in the summer. On Darien Street, the postage-sized backyards were the patios, lawns and decks of today, and were often used for outdoor entertaining in the summer. That they were separated from the alley by a well-worn wooden fence never dampened the festivities. My parents served watermelon and beer on these rare social occasions. Invitations were spontaneous and inclusive. The beer was obtained by seven-year-old me, very carefully carrying a glass pitcher to a bar on Ritner street and exchanging a nickel for a substantial quantity of beer, which I carried home even more carefully. No age restrictions existed for serving minors, or if they did, nobody paid attention.

For the boys, never the girls, there were pinball machines and pool tables, usually in the back room of a corner candy store. These were considered evil pursuits and were discouraged. Discouraged is too mild a word. If evidence existed that a son was seen in such an establishment, punishment was the result. I remember a neighbor coming to my father's barber shop to tell him a sighting was made of my younger brother operating a pinball machine at a store on Oregon Avenue. This was serious. My father locked the barber shop door temporarily, went to the offending site, and physically removed my brother from those evil pinball machines. I wonder, do former South Philadelphians who visit the casinos get a twinge of guilt as they pull the lever on the one-armed bandits?

During World War 11, neighborhoods often held block parties. My memory is that they were a sort of fund raising event for the war effort, but I don't remember how the money was used. There were street lights and music, social opportunities, food and camaraderie. The street was blocked off in the early part of the day to prepare it for the festivities. Neighbors all pitched in to set up booths with sale items, and lights were strung along the rooftops. Adults and kids mingled at these street parties. One of the neighbors contributed a record player turned up to full volume with amplifiers and the jitterbug music and ballads of the day were played over and over again on 78 rpm records. People looked forward to those block parties, and, after the war some neighborhoods attempted to revive them for other causes, but the fired-up enthusiasm was over.

For nascent teenage girls, a major topic of conversation was boys. The question always was: How do you get a boy you like to notice you? The answer was gatherings. Having a gathering meant girls could invite boys to someone's home for an evening of dancing, soft drinks and potato chips without seeming forward. It was not considered aggressive to invite boys to a party. Sometimes gatherings were organized for the specific purpose of getting one couple together to assess whether there were sparks. The girlfriends were in on the plan; the boys were not; at least, we didn't think they were. The gathering could settle once and for all if there was an attraction, or the potato chips were all in vain. As precursors to adult couple dinner parties, these gatherings served as an aperitif to learning how to manage ourselves in social situations. We probably made a lot of awkward mistakes, and the next day the phone lines were busy with rehashes, regrets and recriminations. We often wondered if the boys called each other to discuss the evening. We never knew.

But the ubiquitous entertainment available to all (11 cents for a Saturday matinee for kids) was the movies. Our neighborhood had several theaters, but the one I usually went to on Friday night was The Colonial at 11th and Moyamensing. Friday night was collection night and I was elected by my parents to be the collector. The theaters boasted cumulative giveaways, expecting to produce repeat business. My job at the movies was to collect what became our family's first complete set of china (no pieces missing or chipped-yet) and the set of encyclopedias, red leather binding encasing ivory-colored embossed leather, that I used throughout my school years. The dishes were ivory colored with applique peach -colored roses and gold rims. That set was inter-generational, following my daughter to college and to her first apartment. That was the best job I ever had — a responsibility to go to the movies. Dutifully and happily I went, enthralled by the musicals of John Payne and Betty Gable, sobbing at Bette Davis' imminent demise in "Dark Victory" and thrilled to her unlikely shipboard romance with Paul Heinreid in "Now Voyager." And how many times did I return to see "Seventh Heaven," with that scene in New York's Penn Station, the lovers promising to meet again when the clock struck seven. Was it Robert Walker who waited in vain for Jennifer Jones? And Sonya Heine, spinning, spinning on the ice with such incredible grace. How these movies fueled my romantic fantasies! But to my mother the important result of that evening at the movies was the giveaway.

Movies were at 7 and 9 o'clock. I seem to have always gone to the late show which brought me walking home alone at almost 11 p.m. No one seemed to worry about it, least of all me. With good reason. Nothing ever happened.

Saturday afternoon was reserved for kids, and before my Friday night collecting, Saturday movie matinees with friends were the highlight of the week. No street play or invented games equaled Saturday afternoon at the movies. I waited impatiently for "Gone with the Wind" to make its appearance, and when it did, at the Grand, my mother shared my excitement and we both took a weekday afternoon off, she from the house and me from school, to go see it. I was too impatient to wait for Saturday. We both agreed it was worth playing hooky. Even during summer, when possibilities existed every day to use those hours in whatever way we wished — and had permission — Saturday afternoon was movie time. A big inducement to stay all day was the air conditioning, a first for movie houses. We had possibilities beyond The Colonial. The Grand at 7th and Synder was worth the longer walk and The Ideal, on Sixth street, had a reputation for uncleanliness and was dubbed "The Idump." The Broadway, at Broad and Snyder, was a little further away but often worth the walk. Perhaps the theaters didn't have matinees on other days since Saturday was the day to go, even during the summer when all other days were available. Afternoon may be a misnomer, as going to the movies was an all-day event. We went in groups, starting at about age 7. The more the merrier was apparently the motto. We were accompanied by a brown paper bag, holding lunch, meant to be consumed while watching the movie, and a precious nickel to buy a candy bar at a dispensing machine. There was no popcorn to tempt us, no stands selling soda or hot dogs, only vending machines. One would think that made choices easier, but we could stand for a long time in front of that vending machine, trying to decide between a Goldenberg Peanut Chew or Hershey Kisses. The more adventurous among us bought those delicious salted caramel-coated nuts in a bar, "peanut brittle." The candy bars were dessert for the baloney or tuna fish sandwiches, always on rye bread and often accompanied by a hard boiled egg. A piece of fruit might be included, but no sweet, because there was that nickel, waiting to be spent (or wasted as our mothers always predicted) on the candy of the day.

We didn't just wait for the latest Fred Astaire/Ginger Rogers dance-a-thon, or shiver with unacknowledged passion as Tyrone Power bestowed his chaste kisses on Rita Hayworth. There was lots more to enjoy. Today's trailers were our coming attractions, seductively inviting us to be in the same place at the same time the following week. We needed no inducement. Then there was a full length cowboy movie, Gene Autry or Roy Rogers or Hopalong Cassidy, riding their gallant steeds into the sunset, having successfully foiled the latest cattle rustlers, those mean-spirited and sinister-looking hombres, always with beard-growth and beady eyes. Sometimes the cowboy movie was supplanted by, or better yet, joined by, an adventure film starring the Lone Ranger and his sidekick, Tonto, or Batman and his sidekick, Robin. Then we could see our radio heroes spring to life in front of us, and at the next broadcast, our ears close up against the speaker, we could visualize them as we saw them on the screen. Sometimes the adventure films or cowboy films were in the form of serials, luring us back week by week.

Often, a comedy was included. Robert Benchley, one of the first of the stand-up comics, spouting humor that was probably above our heads in sophistication and contemporary culture. And that wasn't all: Movietone News, "the eyes and ears of the world," apprised us of world events long before we looked to the daily newspaper, with Lowell Thomas' sonorous tones stressing the gravity of his revelations. I've saved the best for last: the cartoon. We were young enough to find the cartoon characters uproarious, and when the little stuttering pig appeared at the end telling us, "That's all folks," we were ready for the main event.

Sometimes there was a double feature and we could stay for yet another hour and a half (in those days movies were prescribed at 90 minutes.) Barring that good fortune, we could, and often did, stay to see the feature movie all over again. No usher came to clear out the seats, no chaperone told us it was time to leave. By the time we did leave, lunch and candy bar consumed, it was evening–the end of an entirely satisfactory day.

Organized after-school sports were non-existent. There were no soccer moms because there was no soccer. But that doesn't mean there was no exercise. Street games were organized by the kids after school. Some sports overcame gender differences. My father made me a scooter when I was about seven years old, which I rode endlessly up and down the street. He also believed, before it was popular, that girls could do the same things boys did, and he decided I should learn how to ride a bike. On his day off, which was Monday, he rented a two wheeler bike from the candy store around the corner. The store had a large display of bikes on the sidewalk, some for sale but most for rental. The cost was 5 cents an hour. My dad spent that hour running behind me, holding the seat to ensure my safety, while his unathletic daughter zigzagged up and down the street. It took an entire summer of Mondays, but I did learn, and wished desperately for a bike of my own. My wish was rewarded. For my 12th birthday I found a beautiful ivory and aqua girl's bike waiting for me, the very one I had coveted with its "for sale" sign outside the candy store. I loved that bike for years, using it as my major means of neighborhood transportation until I was 18, when I reluctantly but proudly gave it to the Haganah in its collection of bicycles for Israel.

During World War 11 the Philadelphia Navy Yard was a major shipbuilding facility and housed many sailors who, with some time off and no vehicle, walked through League Island. This was a park which fronted the Navy Yard and provided a lake (which generated its neighborhood nickname of "the Lakes"), and a lot of grass for picnics and lazy afternoons. When darkness descended, a Lover's Lane was in place at the Lakes. After I had my precious bike, I took long rides, solo, to the Lakes. As a young teenager, I was both nervous and thrilled when a sailor whistled at me, and grateful for the speed my bike gave me to get away.

Without the electronic pastimes we enjoy today, children, especially, were dependent on sparse community offerings and their own imagination for entertainment and amusement. One was the neighborhood library, always available with helpful librarians who shushed us constantly and did not yet offer story book hours or help with homework but supervised the children's choices with a critical eye. I remember being chastised for taking too many books at one time, and when I pleaded to take books meant for children in a higher grade, I was told an emphatic "no." In the summer, the library was cool and refreshing. The stacks offered endless possibilities to get lost in "Nancy Drew" or "The Bobbsey Twins." I sometimes chose a book, cloistered myself at one of the long tables and immersed myself in the tantalizing pages until I finished it. That meant I could return to the stacks and choose a replacement to take home. I also remember trudging to the library at Broad and Ritner with snow piled at the curb up to my head, worried about dropping a library book deep into the snow drift and being unable to retrieve it. Not available at the library but in abundance at corner candy stores and in my father's barber shop were comic books. They must have eased the way for many a slow reader. Most of today's super heroes had their beginnings in the pages of Marvel Comics and Monster Comics and the many other publishing companies that satisfied kids' tastes for vicarious adventure.

These brave and courageous defiers of crime and corruption were everywhere: in comic books, in movie serials, in newspaper cartoon strips, and, to our delight, in radio serials. We listened to their adventures avidly, and the producers were kid-wise, and broadcast them after school, available for listening in that hiatus between school and homework.

More for the girls, other daytime serials could be heard when home from school for lunch, accompanied by a tuna fish sandwich or dinner leftovers. We followed their lives and discussed their options. The two I remember vividly were "Our Gal Sunday" and "Helen Trent." Sunday was a girl from the Midwest who married a wealthy and titled Englishman, Lord Henry Brinthrop, and the big issue was if this naive young woman could adapt to the life of the English aristocracy. The focus of Helen Trent was of a more recognizable nature: Could a woman find happiness past the age of 30? Happiness meant a husband, of course.

Saturday mornings offered more child-oriented radio entertainment. Saturday was my stay-in-bed late morning, and as I opened my eyes, I turned on my bedside radio. "Let's Pretend" dramatized familiar fairy tales with the introductory music that of "Country Gardens" by Percy Granger. More serious fare followed with "Grand Central Station, Crossroads of a Million Private Lives." Before television, Sunday night was family entertainment on the radio, and we all sat around this rounded brown box laughing uproariously at Jack Benny, Fred Allen, George and Gracie, and the litany of comics who brightened our evenings and provided a wholesome experience for the entire family.

The introduction of television into homes completely changed the recreational habits of all people, not only South Philadelphians. Radio was a passive entertainment; listeners could continue to do whatever needed doing — washing dishes, iron, making dinner, painting a chair, fashioning a workbench, even reading a newspaper with the soft buzz of sound a soothing accompaniment. But television required active participation. You had to be in one place and engage several senses. Perhaps it brought families closer together. Certainly it created a new and varied topic of discussion for everyone. "Did you watch...?"

All beginner sets were black and white, relatively small, producing a fuzzy picture, but this invention changed the lives of so many. This didn't, at first, challenge the predominance of movies, but evenings spent watching Sid Caesar in "The Show of Shows," or Milton Berle in "The Texaco Star Theater" created an entire new avenue of entertainment and conversation. Before color TV, people bought plastic shields with three bands of primary colors and placed them over the screen which produced an even fuzzier non-resemblance to color.

New York's Second Avenue with its abundant offerings of Yiddish Theater was not very accessible. Philadelphia did have the Arch Street Theater, and sometimes a road show from Second Avenue made its appearance there, a welcome and highly anticipated event. But the Philadelphia Jewish community did have Yiddish films, and several movie houses, mostly on Girard Avenue, specialized in these films. The titles of some of them will have a familiar ring: "A Letter to Mother," "The Dybbuk," "Green Fields," which featured Herschel Bernardi, "The Cantor's Son," a film based on the life of Moishe Oysher in which he starred, and "Little Mother," instrumental in the blossoming career of Molly Picon.

For a short time a friend of my parents' owned one of these theaters, and because of my special status as child of the friend of the owner, I was allowed into the projection room. I don't remember the Yiddish film, but I remember a short subject, in English, of an actor wandering slowly through a lush forest reciting Joyce Kilmer's poem, "Trees."

Dinner parties and cocktail parties were non-existent. Sometimes extended families gathered for a holiday meal but that was the extent of social entertaining. On a special occasion shot glasses might appear for a swallow of Four Roses, but that began and ended social drinking. It wasn't until I saw movies featuring a living room with a chrome and glass tea cart against a wall as a setting for an ice bucket, cocktail glasses and bottles of liquor, that I concluded this was how residents of Park Avenue and Sunset Boulevard lived — a far cry from South Philadelphia.

CHAPTER THREE

Joining To Stick Together

I was a joiner. My memories of elementary school have as much to do with girls' clubs as with classrooms. Joining organizations was true of many neighborhood families. Whether social, political, financial, or for that matter, any excuse, groups were formed, had meetings (which meant someplace to go) and much leisure time was spent in organizational activities. Amid a politically aware family and my parents' friends, it was inevitable that I, too, would be politically directed, and as a young teenager this direction took the form of fervent Zionism.

Across from my father's barber shop was a hardware store owned by Mr. Morgenstein. I never knew his first name. All my parents' contemporaries were addressed as Mr. or Mrs., by children, (and sometimes by each other) and to this day I never knew his or his wife's first name. As in most "mom and pop" stores, Mr. and Mrs. Morgenstein lived behind and above their store with their two teenage daughters. They were older than I by four and six years, and there was an adult son, already out of the home. The younger daughter, known by her Hebrew name, "Tzip," shortened from Tzipora, was in high school when she and I became friends. Her sister, Naomi, was already working. Both girls were ardent Zionists and recruited me, a willing and eager participant.

I threw all my teenage passion into this movement. My mother approved. She liked Tzip and Naomi; they were intellectuals, and I think my mother thought it was high time I developed whatever nascent intellectual capacity she hoped was dormant in me. And intellectuals they were. On summer nights the two young women sat outside with friends, expounding lofty ideas of politics and philosophy. I was often invited to join them and never felt un-welcome. We sat on the front steps that led to the entrance to the hardware store, the coolness of the concrete a welcome balm to the summer evening's stagnant humidity.

It was at one of these summer evening gatherings that I heard of the novel "Jean-Christophe" by the French author Romain Rolland. The next day I was at the library, requesting it, and mak-ing a valiant but unsuccessful attempt to start reading this ten volume opus. Sometimes at these evenings (I like to think of them as a "salon,") I heard some unfamiliar vocabulary I didn't un-derstand. One word I remember was "repulsive." I tucked these words into my head, and the moment I walked across the street to my house I ran to our red, leather bound unabridged dictionary, and looked up the word. My vocabulary increased dramatically that summer, although fortunately I was never asked to use "re-pulsive" in a sentence. The political ideas I heard opened a world to me I had learned about vaguely in history books, but not with any great interest. Now, my curiosity was piqued, my emotions stirred, and I spent the rest of my teenage years seeking answers to universal questions, joining and discarding all sorts of groups espousing radical political philosophies, and joining a picket line wherever I found one.

The summer I was thirteen I started to accompany Tzip and Naomi to Hashomir Hatzair meetings, which was then, and still is, an organization devoted to a socialist political structure in Israel. The talk was all about everyone's intent eventually to settle in what was then "Palestine," before the State of Israel was a reality. These young people talked of being "chalutzim," pioneers who would settle the land with hard work, farming and building. Some eventually did. I was willing to join them, even though I didn't know a hoe from a plough. After meetings, we went down to League Island to dance Israeli dances and sing Hebrew songs. I was exhilarated. The young men and women were voracious in their cause and I joined in their dedication with great zeal.

The organization sponsored a summer camp outside of Baltimore, in Jones Station, MD. The camp was situated on a large lake. I was allowed to go for two weeks. Overnight camp was not an option for families in our neighborhood. I had known only one contemporary, a relative, who went to overnight camp so this was a thrilling experience for me. In summers, the streets were our camp. This was my first overnight camp experience, and my last, which had nothing to do with my appreciation of the time spent there. I loved those two weeks. What my parents didn't realize, and were subsequently never told by me, was that the camp was run entirely by teenagers and a few young people approaching their early twenties. A few 18, possibly 19 year-olds, were the seniors. I was the youngest camper and celebrated my 13th birthday during my two week stay. My cabin consisted of five 13 to 15 year old girls. Our counselor, Aryeh, was a 19-year-old, handsome blue-eyed blonde from Brooklyn. A boy! As this was my first camp experience, I had no idea how unusual it was to have a male as a counselor in a girls' bunk. I suppose sex was in the air, or more concrete, for the older teenage campers, but in our bunk, despite the presence of this handsome young man, sex was not discussed. Innocence was the name of the game.

My world changed during those two weeks. No adults around meant self-responsibility. That challenge seemed to be met by all campers, including me. The camp had a library which I wandered into the first day. Until then my reading, though voracious and important to me, consisted mainly of kids' series, teen adventures, school assignments, and similar ilk. In the camp library I stumbled upon and arbitrarily checked out Norwegian Knut Hamsun's "Growth of the Soil." I took it by chance, probably curious about the title and that it was a translation from a foreign language. What an eye-opener! From that moment, my reading thirst was slaked by more mature, more far-ranging literature. Goodbye Nancy Drew, hello literature.

That novel was a revelation for me. I suppose it must have been the first mature book I ever read. I learned subsequently that Hamsun received the Nobel Prize for Literature, and much to my dismay, also learned that he was an admirer of Hitler and a supporter of the Nazi party in Norway.

My two weeks at camp, "Moshevah," as we called it, affected me profoundly. The myopia of my child's vision faded and was replaced with an awareness of world issues, of subtleties of relationships, of desires beyond self-improvement and gratification. When I returned from this camp experience, I believe I was on the track for maturity.

During the latter years of elementary school, the need for socialization increased as we little girls started to leave childhood. Without the diversions of television, malls, video games, and the panoply of recreation available to kids today, we had more time for what would be called "interpersonal relationships." In other words, we talked to each other. I'm not sure about pre-teen boys, but for girls this took the form of clubs. We formed a club for everything and often without any purpose except an excuse to be together and talk. We talked about our teachers, about books we were reading, about movies and movie stars, about kids we knew, both male and female. I doubt if these conversations were recip-rocated by our male peers. When I and my girlfriends were 11, the boys we knew were still little kids, all of them shorter and skinnier than we. We were at the threshold of adolescence with hormones beginning their escalation; the boys were shooting marbles and having fist fights over comic books.

Our clubs were highly exclusionary. We voted in every member and had no compunctions about voting someone out. Best friends could be destroyed and new alliances formed within a 15 minute conversation. We voted on everything, from the kind of candy served at a meeting to who wore the prettiest barrette. We had no scruples about making judgments or thinking about "fairness." One subject was never up for discussion; that was family matters. We were cautioned at home never to discuss family issues, to which we were always privy, to any outsider. We had not yet reached the teenager's need to criticize her mother, so that relationship was still sacred.

Fortunately, that phase of togetherness didn't last long and we soon graduated to more serious and substantially more personally beneficial societies. For me, in addition to the already described political groups, it was B'nai B'rith Girls, with access to its male equivalent, AZA (Aleph Zadik Aleph), both groups comprising the youth membership of the international B'nai B'rith Organization. I joined when I was 13 and remained an involved member until my sophomore year in college. That organization was pivotal to the rest of my life in many ways. I met interesting and intelligent young women from all parts of the country, attended national conventions in New York and St. Louis and Detroit and other places I would never have had a reason to seek out at that age. I cut my teeth in public speaking, understood the value of adults, both professional and lay, who devoted their time, energy and professional lives to mentoring youngsters. And, the icing on the cake, I met my future husband when I was 16 through AZA.

But the mainstay of the South Philadelphia neighborhood conversation and argument was politics. Although few people actually aligned themselves with a political organization, most felt passionately about issues. As working-class people who had jobs or small businesses they were all Democrats. The focal point of the neighborhood was the committeeman, and in our district, Division 1, Ward 39, he was Manny Weinberg. Manny was a mild-mannered man with an often dour expression, no doubt due to the many, and sometimes impossible, requests he received for favors from his constituents. They ranged from fixing a traffic ticket to finding a job for a newly imported relative. On Monday nights he held court in the living room of his home where neighbors could wait their turn and make their requests. Manny was more important than the ordinary "ward heeler," so reviled in political literature. He was a member of the Philadelphia City Council, which increased respect for him and it was hoped increased his ability to grant favors.

In 1924, Manny was a young man just starting his long tenure in local politics. But his interests went beyond South Philadelphia and he supported the third party candidate Robert La Folette who ran for president that year on the Progressive Party ticket, a party he formed himself. La Follette was a senator from Wisconsin who, like Fritz Mondale many years later, won only his state. In addition, probably much to national puzzlement, he won the 39th ward in South Philadelphia, where Manny's constituents dutifully voted for his chosen candidate.

But politics went beyond the ordinary conventions of Democrats and the rare Republican. Everyone argued politics, from Socialism and Communism to local issues and national elections. South Philadelphians understood the privilege of the vote and election days found lines in front of the shabby voting booths. Even though I was 21, the legal voting age at that time, I was so excited about my first vote I couldn't sleep, and was first in line when the polls opened.

What a dilemma the Stalin-Hitler treaty of 1939 created! Many sentimental Communists (few ever actually joined the Party) were devastated and many arguments over tea and Mandelbrot took place. More than world chaos resulted; families and friends duplicated that muddle around the kitchen table, taking sides and arguing heatedly. One of my very first memories, as a young child, was hearing an argument between my mother and a family friend, both through clenched teeth, Joe arguing that the Hitler/Stalin pact would be of benefit to the Soviet Union, and my mother haranguing him (this was 1939) about the dangers of Hitler and what it would mean for the Jews of Germany. Very few anticipated then the effect on the Jews of all of Europe.

Of course, with the trickling of information about the Holocaust and the entrance of the United States into the war, arguments stopped and all pulled together. Once information about Stalin's viciousness emerged, many disgruntled leftists were dismayed. Not only was their idealism shattered, they were left without a political cause to defend.

No organization, no matter how emotionally laden and sentimental its origins, equaled the intensity of political affiliations. My father's barber shop was a natural venue for political discussion, most often arguments, and many times I worried about the voices raised above the water running in the shampoo sink and the snip snip of the scissors.

There were no Republicans, only variations of Democrats and moves along the left wing continuum. If any connection could be made union membership was an obligation. Although my Dad was a shop owner, he belonged to the Barbers' Union forever and proudly displayed his union plaque on the wall of the shop.

No matter what dot on the spectrum anyone supported, everyone loved Franklin Roosevelt. The day he died was a day of abject mourning in South Philadelphia. My parents draped a black ribbon around his photograph and displayed it on the wall of the shop for months. It took a long time for the Jews of South Philadelphia to feel that connection with another president.

For my parents, their most important affiliation was the Zhitomirer Beneficial Association, anglicized to "Zitomir." This was the city of origin for my father and his family. It is located in Ukraine, and is now a vibrant city. When my grandparents lived there, it was much more rural, especially where the Jewish population lived. When my grandfather and some of his "landsleit" (folks from the same neck of the woods) came to the U.S., they, just as many similar groups did, formed an organization of contemporaries. The primary reason was to assure Jewish burial so one of their first tasks was to buy cemetery ground. Burial societies provided that avenue. They assured ritual Jewish burial and also created social opportunities. " Landsmanshaft," the organizations they created , were the natural vehicle to get this process underway. But they needed land for graves. Ghoulish as it may sound, these burial organizations provided the familiarity that these new and confused immigrants needed to assure them that some things remained familiar.

My grandfather helped found the Zitomir Beneficial Association, which did what so many other similar organizations did: they bought land far from the city where ground was plentiful and cheap. But probably a more important reason for this affiliation was the familiarity of people they knew, with the same memories, to satisfy that empty hole of homesickness, especially when most of the men came without their families, hoping to earn the money to send for them sometime in the future.

These organizations grew to include people not born in that town; indeed, people not even from another country. Their social events flourished and included annual banquets and many charitable events. In these fraternal organizations, the wives were not actual members but were part of the "Ladies Auxiliary." They met as a separate entity with their own officers and agenda, which was focused on being a satellite of the men's group, the premier organization. The Ladies' Auxiliary had its own functions, usually fund-raisers with the bounty raised contributed in a formal ceremony to the men's group, who, in turn, contributed it, with a combined fund of their own collection, to a charity. I think it did not occur to the women that having raised funds on their own, it was their right to disburse it themselves to a cause of their choosing. They functioned as a separate organization except for the major goal, which was to be the support of the men's group.

Eventually, women, somehow sensing their ability to run an organization on their own, would be instrumental in forming charities that raised enormous sums to support social service agencies, hospitals, homes for the aged, children's orphanages. Perhaps it was their apprenticeship as collateral to men's organizations that gave them the courage to organize and flourish on their own.

Although my family familiarity was with the Zitomir 'farein," (organization) many similar groups existed for the same purpose: originally to provide appropriate burial, and then for companionship and familiarity. Some names that come to mind, in addition to Zitomir, are Pannonia and Breslover, although there were others. An element of competition was bound to exist, and it did. Number of members was a factor, and perhaps the luxury of their annual banquets. Eventually, of course, these organizations faded from the scene. They always spoke of getting "new blood," but the new blood would be the children or grandchildren of original members, for example, my generation. We had our own groups to join, and certainly would have balked at participating in what we would have seen as "European old-fashioned clatches." And the reality is, generations have different social needs, so the once flourishing "landsmanshaft" fraternities fizzled out, but had an important impact on the ease of immigrants shifting into a new way of life in America.

No doubt today's Asian immigrants, with family businesses and loyalties, have evolved similar societies for help and socialization.

Synagogues were a place to pray and mark life cycle events; they did not supply the social glue they do today, so men's clubs and sisterhoods were not part of the social fabric of the community. Groups gathered for social exchanges during weddings and bar-mitzvahs, during holiday commemorations and other religious experiences, but the facility itself was not used as a social hall. Today, with a more intact idea of community, synagogues are utilized as gathering places for all kinds of community events and experiences, including non-Jewish groups as well.

I doubt that organizational affiliations existed in any formalized way in the shtetls or cities from which that generation emigrated. Certainly the fear of assembly was present and the most serious efforts were dedicated to self-preservation, physically and economically. The opportunity to convene, to organize, to talk freely, to argue without fear of retribution, were rewards enough for taking this major step in their lives.

At the annual banquets, often the highlight of member's social activity of the year, a bottle of liquor was served at every table. My dad, not a great connoisseur of libations, believed in accumulating the bottles and saving them for the next event. But he didn't want an excess of bottles, so at the end of the evening, he poured from one bottle to another so that only a few filled bottles remained. This would have been perfectly reasonable and efficient except -the bottles contained a variety of liquor: rye, scotch, etc.

That was just my father's way of serving his organization. To him, and to many members, this was their avenue for a social life, for friendships and alliances. Groups of like-minded people have always served that function, gathering together for pleasure in each other's company was their lifeline for friendship and solidarity.

The liquor was donated by those funeral directors who were members of the organization. As the population of the organization aged, the funeral directors assumed a prominent role. Their contribution of the liquor to the annual banquet was their way of establishing status in the organization,. Today, we might call it "pr" or "networking."

CHAPTER FOUR

Money:
It's Always A Worry

No one in South Philadelphia knew much about stock markets, options, investments, or what to do with excess cash. Few people had excess cash. Most were service workers or independent contractors: paperhangers, house painters, plumbers, carpenters, and the like. They were what we might call "freelancers," or, in today's parlance, subcontractors, working alone, hopeful that one job would lead to another. Others, like my father, were proprietors of small neighborhood businesses at street corners or on Seventh Street, the commercial hub of the neighborhood. What people earned each week was usually what they had to spend the following week on life's everyday costs.

Almost all corner stores or store front businesses on Seventh Street were part of the family's home, which was reconfigured to accommodate the business. The kitchen was usually just behind the store, so that the wife could be available to help when the husband/owner had more than one customer or was away for some reason. The woman emerged from the kitchen, often drying her hands on a perpetually donned-apron, while the aroma of whatever was on the stove followed her, wafting into the store.

Home ownership was for the future, so most families rented, always worried about an increase or whether the owner might choose to sell. Often, that circumstance forced the renters to borrow or rearrange their resources so that they could manage a down payment and get a mortgage. If a family lived in a house long enough to pay off their mortgage, there was often a literal mortgage burning ceremony.

Because my father had a service business, both he and my mother felt obliged to patronize his customers who had retail businesses: tit for tat. So even though Sam's market might have fresher produce, if Sam's sartorial splendor was achieved in a barber shop other than my father's, we had to patronize Sam's competitor, my Dad's customer. I took this admonition very seriously, and when I was sent on a shopping errand, I didn't need to be told in which store to shop. I knew. What I didn't realize was that there were exceptions that had to do with stores that couldn't possibly produce customers for my father. So when my mother and I shopped at Gimbel's, and then crossed Market street to ferret out the bargains at Lit Brothers, I carefully turned the Gimbel's bag so that their logo could not be seen by the salespeople at Lits.

Saturday night was counting night at our house. Dad's store closed about 9 p.m. when he opened the cash register. All income was deposited in this old-fashioned and ornate register as soon as the customer paid. Every time the drawer was opened, a bell sounded, a welcome ring to my mother in the kitchen. My father emptied the week's take on the linoleum-topped kitchen table and the accounting began. My father counted the paper money, my mother got to stack the quarters, I did the dimes and my brother the nickels. The process didn't take very long. The bills and change, now in neat piles on the kitchen table, was the largesse of the week, and the sum of the earnings totaled our family's spendable income for the following week. I remember feeling proud that I was included as part of the counting process, but I'm sure I had no sense of the limitation of earnings or its dependence. As times grew better, my parents opened a checking account at a local bank. Until then, my parents, as did all the neighbors, paid utility bills in person at the neighborhood bank. Not many people had bank accounts; banks were visited mostly for loans, mortgages, or to pay bills. But the bankers understood there was a future to be tapped in this society and in a brilliant PR gesture, PSFS, The Philadelphia Saving Fund Society, issued passbooks to school children to encourage saving, with the cooperation of the schools. These passbooks were distributed in the classroom, and that's where deposits were made — deposits accepted even in small coins.

We children were proud of the accumulation in our passbook, and no addition seemed too small to us then. Years later, when the State of Pennsylvania began publishing, as they still do, long lists in the newspapers of persons who had lapsed savings accounts in banks, monies that will revert to the State if they are not claimed in a prescribed period of time, those small amounts in PSFS accounts appear with predictable regularity on those lists, passbooks long forgotten in abandoned bureau drawers or coat pockets.

With household costs and other expenses dependent on daily receipts, few families had disposable income. For those heads of households who had regular jobs working for a company or a store (always men; married women did not work outside the home), the income was steadier, though laced with the constant threat of job loss overriding the dependable paycheck. Sudden needs for extra cash created a dilemma. Few people had resources that qualified them for bank loans, and loan companies were objects of suspicion and thought to be usurious. Emergencies or down payments on houses were often met by borrowing money, either from a "rich" relative or the "Corporation." Although a legal name was registered with the state, I never heard it called anything but "the Corporation." The Corporation was just that, a legally established loan company registered with the state of Pennsylvania and empowered to lend money and collect interest. For many families, this financial lifeline made an immediate and compelling difference in their lifestyle.

This is how it worked: members paid nominal dues and had the privilege of borrowing money at a set interest rate, probably somewhat higher than prevailing interest rates, but borrowers did not have to submit credit statements or references. Their word was their bond and they were all known to their neighbors and members of the Corporation. My parents belonged to the neighborhood Corporation, whose members all lived "just around the corner." I suspect that was the source of funds to finance my wedding. Meetings were held once a week where verbal applications were considered and approved and sealed with a handshake. I don't know if there were any defaults, but that would certainly have been an active avenue for gossip and disapproval. There was no such thing as privacy in the Corporation. Even a late payment was a disgrace. The threat of gossip was minimal compared to the comfort level of dealing with friends and neighbors, all of whom were empathic in a financial crisis.

This organization was probably an outgrowth of the old burial societies which immigrants established to make certain that Jews, no matter how poor, had a decent burial. These financial groups existed to "help out" in times of distress or need or want. We could probably compare them, with an escalating difference in interest rates, to today's credit cards where people use the credit card for both essentials and frivolities and pay the interest rate and principal within a designated time frame. In conversation with Italian friends, I find their immigrant families had an identical method of lending money within their community. It's also my understanding that contemporary Asian immigrants, trying to establish themselves in business, use a similar method of borrowing and repayment.

An urban legend has it that a national bank started as a South Philadelphia neighborhood Corporation expanded to become a corner Savings and Loan on Seventh Street. Once it became a real bank, the president and founder of the Corporation became an esteemed member of the community. The neighborhood Corporation presidents had the status of today's CEO, with power on a significantly lower scale. Nonetheless, this was a position of respect. The Corporation supplied funds for anything from a week's vacation in Atlantic City to the down payment on a new house. I doubt there was ever a family social event that was not supported, in part, by a loan from the Corporation. An apocryphal cartoon story makes the rounds that depicts a South Philadelphia matron, splashing water at herself at the juncture of the surf and the sand on an Atlantic City beach while she murmurs, "God bless the Corporation."

How money was apportioned within the family depended on the family dynamics and who had responsibility for what. As women had no independent income, they were dependent on their husband's generosity for any private spending money. Some wives handled all the husband's earnings to run the household and do with whatever they deemed necessary; others got an "allowance" out of which household expenses were portioned out. All these methods left little for personal extravagance. Inherited from European shtetl society came the "knippl" method of women's private savings. In Yiddish, knippl means "knot," and the old world assumption was that any small change that could be squirreled away from family necessities could be secreted in a handkerchief and a knot tied to secure the stash. This was private female money, hidden away to accommodate fantasy longings for a pair of silk stockings or even to give to a needier relative.

Money was always a problem. When things were tight, and in

the '30s they always were, groceries could be charged at the corner store. A primitive precursor to credit cards, tabs were kept on brown paper bags by the proprietor, and items and accompanying amounts were added to the column as they accrued. As soon as a paycheck came, or a job was finished, the grocer was the first to receive his due. Also in line were the men collecting for items bought on the installment plan. This was a typical way to make purchases; everyone used this method. I hesitate to call the men who came to collect the weekly payments "collection agents" because they weren't dunning people; they merely were collecting for items that had been purchased "on time."

Purchases made on this time payment plan were usually large items, such as furniture or appliances, and buyers paid on the balance each month with a considerable interest fee, part of the original loan. The usual repayment was at the rate of 50 cents a week. Essentials such as insurance were always paid out on time, as well as items considered educational or cultural enhancements, such as sets of encyclopedias, radios and record players. The collectors were a neighborhood fixture, and no one was embarrassed by their weekly presence at the front door because everyone used this method for major purchases.

My family's collection agent was Mr. Fleischman, and I believe our time payment was for insurance. He quickly became a friend and confidante, stopping in for a cup of tea as he collected his weekly 50 cents. My parents called him a "real gentleman," which was the highest compliment that could be paid, especially where finances were concerned.

Children were indoctrinated early on the necessity of earning "spending" money. One way was to hang out at the corner drug store and answer the public phones. Several enclosed booths, equally divided between the two telephone companies, Bell and Keystone, stood next to each other, tall and narrow, sometimes outside the store, sometimes inside. Called "phonies," they provided an easy nickel as a tip as many homes did not have private telephones. When a phone rang in the bank of telephones at the corner candy store or drug store, we kids sprang into action. The caller identified the neighbor he or she wanted, and we messengers, who knew all the neighbors, sprinted to the house to summon the person being called, certain of a five cent tip, the cost of a phone call in those days. That was one source of spending money. Another was the return of soda bottles, which always required a deposit of one or two cents at purchase–not too different from today, when street people scavenge trash cans to retrieve cans and bottles and then turn them in to recycling centers for some small amount of cash. We always considered these returns a bonus, because even if the bottles came from our own family's collection, we were usually allowed to keep the return of a few pennies. The All-American custom of young boys delivering newspapers was a frequent source of earning power, and parents also thought early rising was good discipline.

Reward money for the children was confusing. Accepting a "tip" for calling someone to the phone was a respectable way to earn some spending money. Accepting money from parents' friends or relatives was not. I was taught to say politely "no thank you" when such a gift was offered. But then came Chanukah, before the days of eight nightly gifts. When offered Chanukah gelt (money) from the very same people I had to refuse the rest of the year, I was urged to accept. It took years for me to sort this out. Economy within the home was practiced by all. A serious transgression was leaving lights on in an unoccupied room. This discovery resulted in a resounding, "Do you think we have shares in the electric company?" For those families who had phones, phone signaling was one way to save a few pennies with the additional idea that maybe we were fooling the company by outsmarting them.

The phone company provided a variety of services, several types offering money-saving opportunities. If a family had "limited" service, which meant a restriction on the number of calls they could make per month without additional charge, and a relative or acquaintance had "unlimited" service, the household with the limited service signaled the other party — a prearrangement of one or two rings — and the person with the unlimited service returned the call, and there was no extra charge for anybody. It was a far cry from direct dialing for long distance or phone credit cards. A long distance call generated anxiety. Who would spend that extra money unless to report an emergency? As soon as the operator reported "long distance," a cry went up from whoever answered the phone, "Hurry, it's long distance." It was important to get to the phone as soon as possible so that the caller on the other end would incur as few extra time charges as possible, and just as important, to hear the bad news. To this day, I'm sometimes told by the party on the other end of the line after hearing a phone interrupt, "I'll call you back, it's long distance," as if that were the caller's name.

The least expensive method of having a private telephone meant a party line, where the phone line was shared with another family, although ideally one never knew who those people were. No one was every happy with that arrangement. Each member of that party line accused the other partner of hogging the line, staying on too long, giving the children excessive use of the phone, anything that could accuse the other party of being "unfair."

When I was a teenager I was graduated to an allowance, a pittance compared to adolescents' spending habits of today, but enough to keep me in movie gossip magazines. I didn't need much money for cosmetics. Magazines always had ads that asked for a dime or a quarter sent to a well known cosmetic company, and a few weeks later a small packet of samples arrived in the mail for secret experimentation with girlfriends, away from the family. Lipsticks were dark in those days, and I was not permitted this enhancement until I was 14. Even then, as I opened the door to leave with my carmine lips, my father approached me with a tissue every time, announcing "It's too dark," and I was obliged to blot before I could leave the house. Of course, the brightness was reapplied as soon as I reached my friend's house. We favored a brand called 'Chen-Yu." The colors were bright red, housed in an elaborate engraved case. My girlfriends and I all started with a conservative pink gloss called "Tangee."

Business picked up for my father's shop as well as everyone else as World War11 approached and became a reality. My father hired a barber to work the "second chair." But the war also provided opportunities for additional income because workers at the Philadelphia Navy Yard couldn't find lodgings, so we took in boarders, only one at a time. That meant I shared the second bedroom with my brother and the third bedroom (one bathroom for the household) was let out for rent. I only remember two boarders: a young woman and a middle-aged man, not together, of course. The lady made her own bed, but one of my household chores was to make the bed and tidy up the room of the male lodger. I have no recollection of what these renters paid, but it couldn't have added substantially to the cash register. That ended after the war when my uncle, my mother's youngest sibling, came home from the service and moved in with us. He took my place as my brother's roommate, and I finally had my own room. To me it was a holy place. I had a pullout sofa bed so that the room could appear to be a sitting room when I wasn't asleep, also housing a desk, a bookcase and a chair.

As a young teenager, I was ready to begin my many years of a variety of jobs to save money for college. My first salary of $12.00 a week during my 14th summer was earned as a messenger girl at the reception desk of Mt. Sinai Hospital at Fifth and Reed Streets, later to become the Southern Division of Albert Einstein Medical Center, which eventually closed. It was a small neighborhood hospital then. Some of these community hospitals were initially supported by local Jewish agencies such as the Jewish Federation in Philadelphia in the days when quotas and discrimination were rampant.

My responsibilities were varied. I checked in visitors. In those days, visiting hours in hospitals were limited to certain periods of the day and a specified number of visitors for each patient. I had a daily printout of patient's names and rooms, and when visiting hours arrived, I marked off the number of visitors per patient. If additional visitors came beyond the specified two at a time, I called up to the nurses' station to have someone inform the visitors that others were waiting in the lobby. I also distributed mail to patients, took flowers up to rooms, and answered the information line when the receptionist went to lunch. That was the best part of the job because it was the most responsible. Relatives and friends of patients called the information desk to inquire about a patient's condition At the desk we had a daily list from each floor which listed patients' conditions as "good, fair, poor or critical." But we were not permitted to say "critical." If that was the designation, we told the caller to get in touch with the family. I hated to say even "poor," so I preceded that with "I'm sorry to say..."

The hospital switchboard was housed in a small alcove across from the reception desk, separated from the lobby by a curtain. Joe, the day operator, was a burly, lame man with a wonderful speaking voice and a gruff manner that hid his innate kindness. When I was not occupied at the desk, I loved to sit on a stool next to Joe and see him magically manipulate the cords on the cumbersome PBX switchboard. One day he asked me if I would like to learn how to operate the switchboard. I was thrilled to think I might be able to maneuver those snake-like cords successfully. Sometimes I think today's complicated technological push button switchboards are no less challenging. Of course, whenever Joe allowed me to plug in a cord and connect it to the proper party, he was right there to supervise. Occasionally, for a bathroom break, he left me alone to deal with the switchboard, which gave me the foolish self-confidence to think I knew the secrets of a PBX system.

With that experience in mind, I applied for a summer job during my college years to the appliance company Trilling and Montague at 24th and Walnut Streets, and had the audacity to state on my application blank that I could operate a PBX. They hired me. In addition to my clerical duties, part of my job responsibility was to relieve the switchboard operator during lunch. My first day on the job I disconnected Mr. Trilling from Mr. Montague.

I had many jobs before I was graduated from college. Most were part-time clerical positions as a typist or filing clerk, others as a cashier in a children's store, or a dunning clerk for a consignment outlet, and, as I learned more in my journalism classes, I was able to get some writing work that made me feel like a professional. But these jobs paid my tuition, nominal at that time, especially for a commuter student, and I always felt proud that I had "worked my way through college."

CHAPTER FIVE

It's Time To Eat

Dinner parties, cocktail receptions, ladies who lunch and gourmet pizzas were not even wishful thinking. Yet, the preparation and serving of food was the social barometer of the day. When family and friends came to visit, they came to eat. Sometimes it was just tea and homemade cake, sometimes it was a holiday dinner, but food was always part of the equation, a fulcrum on which all ethnic groups revolved. When I visited my junior high school Italian Catholic best friend, Natalina, her parents, unable to communicate in English, offered food. That's how I was introduced to pitzells at Christmas time and home-made wine. Though the wine burned my esophagus and was 360 degrees different from the sweet Passover wine that I was accustomed to, I was too polite to refuse. The pitzells made it worthwhile.

Holiday dinners never varied — appetizer (gefilte fish home made by my aunt if she was in a sharing mode, ordinary baked fish or herring from a jar if she wasn't.) Gefilte fish was always accompanied by red horseradish, the hotter the better. If a taste of it brought tears to one's eyes, the horseradish was declared a huge success. The fish was followed by chicken soup with matzah balls, the soup yellow and oily and delicious, before the days of skimming the fat from the top and leaving the pale, denuded, watery excuse for chicken soup we eat today. The circular globules of fat danced across the top of the liquid, promising smooth passage for the accompanying matzah balls, always referred to by their Yiddish name, "knaidlach." Their presentation brought anxiety to the cook. Were they too heavy, too big, cooked all the way through? No matter. The diners were always appreciative. The brisket came next, roasted to sublime tenderness, which meant falling off the fork into shreds, roasted in a slow oven all day or overnight, canned peas and carrots, potato kugel or potato pancakes or mashed potatoes, or, if we were lucky, sweet noodle kugel. Dessert could be Jell-O, sometimes layered raspberry and lime surrounding canned fruit cocktail, or applesauce accompanied by bakery cookies or my mother's Mandelbrot. She called it "kamish bread," and to this day I don't know if there is a difference between the two, other than language. The hard, crusty crescent shaped cookie always comes to mind when a plate of biscotti is presented at the end of a restaurant meal, or brought to my home as a "hostess gift." I've tried to duplicate the kamish bread but the consistency is never the same, either too cake-like or too crunchy.

Some holidays specialized in offerings that never varied. When my father arrived home from shul at the close of Yom Kippur, orange juice and honey cake awaited him. We always had potato latkes (pancakes) for Chanukah, but Hamantashen for Purim eluded my mother, so they were bought at the corner bakery. Today's sweet fruit fillings are more acceptable than the poppy seed, or "mohn" fillings that seemed the only ones available then. As soon as lekvar (prepared fruit fillings) entered the baking equation, Hamantashen became a year round delicacy. Passover, or "Pesach" as we always referred to this holiday, was character-ized by a friend of mine as a "misogynystic" event. When we cel-ebrated the exodus of the slaves from Egypt, the women took over. Up came the Passover dishes from the basement, needing to be washed and dried, by hand, of course, before the days of dishwashers. Out went the mothers to the stores, buying special Passover foods, planning menus, structuring the Seder nights. Preparing for Passover week often felt like a kinship with those slaves. Even with the help of prepared foods, readily available in supermarkets, this annual commemoration still requires intense preparation. For those families who change dishes and deal with the ritual of cleansing the house of *chumetz* (non-Passover food) the last minute rush can be frantic and exhausting. For those who were kosher, two sets of dishes had to be reclaimed from their storage space, washed by hand, and placed in shelves scoured and emptied of everyday dishes and flatware used the rest of the year.

I remember taking matzah, hard boiled eggs, and a slice of sponge cake, which required twelve eggs for a perfect result, to the high school cafeteria for lunch during the week of Passover. Sometimes sweet macaroons substituted for the sponge cake.

But delectable special Passover foods made the intense prep-arations worthwhile. Fried matzah, potato or matzah meal kugel, sweet desserts, flourless chocolate cake, all were possible to make the rest of the year, but somehow they were all reserved for Pesach.

Shopping was a daily occurrence. This was not because of lack of refrigeration but women considered daily shopping part of their homemaking ritual, and fresh was always better. Stores were all specialty shops. Shopping was also a social occasion. Who else but neighbors would frequent corner stores, so there was always a familiarity that went along with shopping. And the men and wom-en behind the counter were also friends and neighbors. There was no such thing as absentee ownership. All shops were owned and run by a couple, the wife of the family often responsible for any prepared items that were sold, the same foods she cooked in the kitchen for her husband and children. The family often lived on the premises and stores had long hours because, after all, the folks were there anyway. Butcher shops sold meat and poultry; dairy stores sold cheese, butter and milk. Corner grocery stores sold staples and paper goods; produce and fruit were available only in produce and fruit stores. Bakeries offered breads and pastries, all baked on the premises by the owner. Delicatessens sold pickled and smoked meats, and delicatessen-type fish and were busiest on weekends, especially Sunday morning for lox and bagels. People who shunned cooked fish enjoyed smoked and kippered lox, white-fish, salmon, sable, even sturgeon, until it became too expensive a delicacy. Amounts purchased were often small: one quarter pound of corned beef or kippered salmon was not unusual for a family of four. The quantity didn't interfere with customers' instructions to the counterman about how to slice, what to cut off, with a running commentary on the quality of whatever was in the slicer. A count-erman once lamented, "If I could take the fat out of the corned beef and put it into the lox I'd be a millionaire."

No small machines with numbered pull-out tabs on the coun-ters greeted customers at the entrance to the store to determine who should be waited on when. As no stores were self-service, everyone was waited on by someone behind the counter — an unwritten law existed about "nexts." Customers surveyed those before them, memorized their faces or some unspoken physical characteristic, and usually waited their turn in good humor. The humor disap-peared if a customer tried to block someone else's turn.

Some items, not readily available at the corner grocery, such as specialized dairy products, were available in specialty stores. There were two dairy specialty stores on Seventh Street: Saler's and Gittleman's. No pre-packaged products existed on shelves or in refrigerated cases. Butter appeared in long, thick, yellow loaves and each quarter or half pound was sliced off in precise squares. I often marveled at how accurate the countermen were; they seemed never to need to add or subtract a smidgen to get the weight the customer requested. Cheese, too, came in long loaves and slices were shaved off from a hand slicer. Plastic wrapped cheeses were way in the future, as were dairy exotica. American, Swiss and Muenster completed the gamut of available cheeses. Edam, Brie, Monterey Jack, and all creamy cheeses (except Philadelphia cream cheese) were unavailable. Perhaps they existed in upscale neighborhood specialty shops, but on Seventh Street choices were limited not only by availability but by the customers' lack of gourmet experience. Cottage cheese was scooped out of a deep wooden barrel in liquid-free chunks, shoveled out in large white lumps the size of coal from the barrel, often emptied into a paper cone and then wrapped in eggshell colored wrapping paper, waxed on one side. Barrels were a fixture in every food store, harboring not only cottage cheese but sour pickles, sour tomatoes, sometimes herring, and a gamut of delicacies that the wooden staves seemed to enhance.

Kosher butcher stores were common in the neighborhood, offering the same fare with customer determination of quality differences. There were two within a half block of each other on Seventh Street, but the business competition didn't seem to interfere with the friendship of the two families. Most butcher stores did not sell poultry. There were special poultry stores, usually on Seventh Street, with live clucking chickens in cages. On Friday mornings these shops were busy. Women could choose their chicken, live, and then the "shoichet," ritual slaughterer, did his job. Somebody else did the feather plucking, a separate job. How would that be described on a resume, I wonder? The women then took the beheaded chicken home and did their own eviscerating, then covered the parts with kosher salt. Surgery complete, the chicken was ready for boiling.

There wasn't too much exposure to ethnic foods other than

Jewish style except as described by Italian neighbors. Pasta was still called "noodles," and its culinary use was limited to cooked kugels, or a melt in your mouth concoction called "lockshen mit kase," noodles with cheese, consisting of the cholesterol-inspired dish of cooked noodles smothered in melted butter and cottage cheese. Noodles had three shapes: wide, medium or fine, with their choice determined by experience.

A few small supermarkets were beginning to rear their heads. The beginning chains I remember were "American Stores" and "Frankford Markets."

Restaurants were an infrequent extravagance, usually reserved for special occasions. And there weren't many from which to choose. Kosher restaurants were centered around Eighth Street and Girard Avenue, and I remember a dairy restaurant and a Roumanian meat restaurant, diagonally across the street from each other. Of course there were delis, and the corner luncheonettes where we never tired of corned beef. My group frequented Nat's at 8th and Porter. Nat's menu featured a #42 special, a three-tiered sandwich of corned beef, lettuce, tomato, and Russian dressing on rye bread. We always ordered the same thing. I still do if I can make it happen, only now it's called a "corned beef special." Kramer's was at the next corner and featured its own version of this specialty. Feldman's at 4th and Snyder was famous for their malted milk shakes, a creamy thick concoction of mostly ice cream and milk, with a dose of malt added to make it healthy.

Fancier restaurants, the ones with white tablecloths and cloth napkins, where you didn't have to reuse your appetizer fork for the entree, were saved for special celebrations, and there were not too many available with familiar food. The restaurant didn't have to be kosher, but for those families not conscientiously observant, the menu needed to have recognizable selections so diners could feel comfortable. Shoyer's on Arch street featured familiar Jewish-style food, and in the early '50s a restaurant opened in a private home in South Philadelphia near Snyder Avenue. Leibowitz's specialized in garlic-smothered rib steaks, garnished with onions, served with a healthy portion of French fries, sour pickles and tomatoes, and a bottle of siphon seltzer on every table. Private homes seemed always to order a case of seltzer per week and the blue glass or clear bottles graced every dinner table the way water does today. The "seltzer man" was an addition to the tradesmen who approached many front doors.

Not for special occasions but still "eating out," the automat, a novel idea started in Philadelphia, created a wonderful opportunity for hearty, inexpensive food. Horn and Hardart's glass windows that opened after coins were inserted offered desserts and sandwiches, albeit on white bread, while the counters provided hot food. My family did an "H and H" outing every Sunday, limiting our platters to vegetables so as not to eat non-kosher meat. My father had the identical meal every week: vegetable soup, a four vegetable platter, and apple pie. When I was old enough to go with friends, we also ordered vegetable platters. A typical plate consisted of home fried potatoes, macaroni and cheese, vegetarian baked beans and Harvard beets. Little did we know!

Linton's tried another tack to compete. Customers sat at a counter and the food passed by on a conveyer belt. Linton's was the choice for Saturday night after-date coffee and Danish, or for the more adventurous, meaning more pocket money, a late breakfast.

Many individual restaurants within these chains had personalities of their own. The Horn and Hardart at 16th and Chestnut was the only place in that chain featuring waitress service, and items usually cost a nickel more than at the automat. The one on Broad street between Walnut and Locust was dubbed "The Heel" by the intellectual young literati of center city, who used it as a meeting ground to discuss the books they would write as soon as their typewriter was repaired or their vision of the painting on the easel evolved with enough money to buy new brushes. An abundance of talk often resulted in a lifelong delay of creativity. Conversation and coffee lasted until the morning hours, and no one was ever turned away, even those who brought their own tea bags to dunk in a free cup of hot water. One would-be poet added the free ketchup to the hot water and enjoyed "tomato soup."

Although my family stopped changing dairy and meat dishes when I was about ten, we adhered to no meat and dairy mixing, so dinners were either meat or dairy. Friday night was always chicken soup and stewed chicken, so Saturday night was chicken salad. Or, if business was good that week, we splurged on corned beef, buying fresh rye bread at the bakery and the cold cuts from the nearest deli, accompanied by potato salad or cole slaw and, of course, a sour pickle. There wasn't too much variety of choice; dairy dinners were baked fish, almost always flounder, or tuna fish salad. Meat dinners were roast beef or hamburger — occasionally but rarely steak.

Street vendors were not around, and their food would have been suspect anyway. Except for water ice, the only street purchases allowed were soft pretzels. We didn't know that Philadelphia would be famous for them. At South Philadelphia High School for Girls, when in the schoolyard for recess, eager hands reached through the bars of the wrought iron fence to thrust a penny at the pretzel man. Sanitation was not a consideration, and I am convinced that the vendor's unwashed hands and the street soot contributed to the good taste. The pretzel was, of course, smothered with yellow mustard, the same kind that made hot dogs taste so good. No Dijon or spicy brown would have improved the quality.

There was a cafeteria in my elementary school, but I can't imagine why, as the children all lived within a few blocks and went home for lunch where mothers awaited them. Perhaps it was primarily for the teachers. My high school, of course, had a large cafeteria, as there wasn't time to go home for lunch, and the school drew from a much larger geographic area than the elementary school. Friday was Shepherd's Pie day, and other offerings were hot dishes and some sandwiches. Probably many of us brought our own lunch and bought a drink.

Hot dogs were in the future. In my home, hot dogs and baloney were forbidden foods. Even if they were kosher, they were not permissible. "Unhealthy," my mother said. "You don't know what's in them." I eventually bought both surreptitiously when I was on my own. One Passover, as I tested my then emerging Pantheistic notions, I bought a hot dog in a roll at the lunch counter at Green's Five and Ten on the corner of Tenth and Market. The guilt wasn't worth it.

Summer nights were polly-seed extravaganzas. Too hot to sleep, people sat on their steps chatting away the night, hoping for a cool breeze. Endless conversation was accompanied by polly-seeds. It was a ritual: cracking the seed with your teeth, releasing the seed from its pod with those same teeth, and spitting, not throwing, the now emptied pod onto the sidewalk.

The children had contests. Who could spit the farthest? Who cleaned it up? The women, when they periodically swept and washed the sidewalks and the steps. Who swept it away from the street? The street cleaners, who came by more often than South Philadelphians like to admit, sweeping and flushing the street, via the fire hydrants, into the corner sewers.

Dishes collected from the movie houses or other giveaway programs were new acquisitions, making them a bit too fancy to use for every day. They were saved for company, although it was rare that enough were collected to create a whole dinner set. But giveaway dishes weren't the only way to enlarge the plate and glass collection. We never bought drinking glasses. Between jelly jars and Yahrtzeit glasses, (holding memorial commemorative candles, lit on the anniversary of a loved one's death), the cupboards were well equipped with drinking vessels. Jars from herring, pickles, condiments, and such products were never tossed.

They were utilized for storage of leftovers and for the use of those ambitious enough to make jellies, jams and preserved fruit.

Before the days of pizza and Big Macs, there were bagels. Today bagels are as popular as doughnuts, surpassing Danish as a coffee accompaniment. Bagels were a breakfast staple, not only for lox and cream cheese, but as the bread of choice with anything else served. Their production was in view at the bakeries, the round balls of dough gently submerged into vats of boiling water by the white-clothed, sweating bakers in the room with the ovens behind the sales counters.

Before sleek, efficient refrigerators and freezers took residence in kitchens, the ice-box was the modern equivalent of the ice-house and the outdoor storage food shed. These units were often made of lovely wood, with bright metal latches, probably chrome. The ice was on the top shelf, where freezers are often found today and naturally, those items that needed the most cold to stay fresh were placed nearest the ice. But ice melts and water drips, so underneath each ice box was a large pan, called a "shissel," and it was often the job of the children in the family to empty the shissel daily. Early refrigerators were of white porcelain with the cooling unit on the top, consisting of a tall circle of coils. Moisture still accumulated so the shissel remained in use until the more modern refrigerators became "frost free."

The closest approximation to "serving drinks" was a shot of whiskey to mark a joyous event. Shot glasses were the only drink glasses in the cabinet, except for the recycled jelly jars and yahrtzeit glasses used for water. The whiskey was Four Roses; more sophisticated families learned of Canadian Club and had a bottle of that around for a few years. The whiskey was served straight up; the men swallowed one shot in one gulp and the women drank nothing hard. Their participation in the drinking ritual was a glass of seltzer, not club soda, served from the siphon bottle.

Condiments were few but were staples. Ketchup was ubiquitous, used on everything from steak to scrambled eggs. My mother's friend Rose dribbled some into her chicken soup. Yellow mustard, sour pickles, mayonnaise — that was pretty much it. Salt and pepper began and ended the seasonings shelf. Before the days of frozen vegetables, what was served was either canned or fresh, and there often was not too much of a choice of fresh vegetables at the produce/fruit store. Green beans, cabbage and peas pretty much sufficed.

Soup was a staple, and for a long time was served in our house as a second course, after the meat or fish entree. That was European style, or at least the Russian habit, and, although my mother was American-born she served dinner this way until we did some exploratory restaurant dining and discovered soup before the entree was the "American" way.

Soups were limited in variety and always good: chicken soup served on Friday nights and on holidays, vegetable soup and split pea at other times. In the summer my mother made sorrel soup, which we called "schav," green and cold and delicious with a dollop of sour cream. It is my understanding that today it is considered a great delicacy. Sometimes beet borscht, also cold, was served in the summer, also with sour cream.

I never remember seeing any recipe books in my home or that of any of my parents' friends. Women seemed to believe that cooking skills were a natural attribute of every housewife, just as I believe they assumed, in those days, that parenting skills emerged with the expulsion of the placenta. My mother, considering herself a modern woman, clipped recipes from women's magazines, which she read prodigiously. The clippings accumulated, and through them we had meatloaf with a hard-boiled egg in the center, or, even more creatively, a canned half peach to surprise us as we sliced the loaf. But what to do with the rest of the half peaches in the can? There they were, shimmering their orange pas de deux in the middle of the slithering Jell-O.

Our family also had the women's magazines to thank for pineapple upside-down cake, chicken fricassee, and mock blintzes, made with sweetened cottage cheese loosely packed between two soda crackers and fried. A bit dry, but tasty.

I marvel today at the variety of prepared foods, both frozen and fresh, available at supermarket counters and specialty stores. I doubt they would have had much of a market in the South Philadelphia of my childhood.

Sometimes life-cycle events were celebrated in the home: a *bris*, a *ben zucha*, a *pedi na ben,* a baby naming; all events commemorating the birth of a child, as well as other joyful occasions, such as a child's graduation, an engagement party, etc. Most of these parties would have been held in the family home, and the cooking and serving and clean-up attended to by the women in the family. Catering was for events that took place outside the home, reserved for serious celebrations such as weddings and bar-mitzvahs. Hiring a caterer for a home event was unheard of and would have jettisoned the family into another economic and social sphere. Home cooking was celebrated and appreciated. Rarely would a caterer be hired for an event in a home.

I don't remember much in the way of prepared foods availability. If they did exist in the refrigerated cabinets of delis or grocery stores, they probably would have been mistrusted as to ingredients and cleanliness of preparation. Anyway, homemade food would always have been declared "better tasting and better for you."

With few funds available for recreation or vacations, impromptu social gatherings became the recreation for most families. And food covered all bases. It showed hospitality, brought out the best in the "balaboosta," (the exemplary housekeeper), and served all as an avenue for news, gossip, conjecture, and compliments, all accompanied by the gastronomic specialties of the household.

Seventh Street, "*die zibiter*" in Yiddish, which is how most people referred to that shopping mecca, was lined with mom and pop stores and providing all food necessities, and a range of purchases from candy to major appliances.

Like all families with limited resources, and limited entertainment opportunities because they still didn't exist, food was the glue that cemented social gatherings, whether for a lifecycle occasion or an impromptu neighborhood get-together. Without the media sources available for recreation today, and without the funds to pursue them even if they had already been created, gathering around a table, laden with familiar foods, commenting on their tastiness (the hostess feebly protesting "not as good as last time"), social activity for family and friends was completely satisfactory.

CHAPTER SIX
School Days

In my elementary school, and probably all others, there were three groups in each grade: The high achievers were in group 1, the average performers in group 2, and all others, those children considered social and emotional misfits, troublemakers, learning disabled, retarded, and even handicapped, or whoever didn't fit a mold, or danced to the tune of a different drummer, were tossed together in group 3. This was called O.B. class, which stood for "orthogenic backward," a label difficult to get expunged from a child's record.

Before the advent of political correctness and the assumption that all children could be successful if only opportunities were equalized, and intelligence testing was determined unfair and possibly obsolete, we children were tracked in school according to what was considered our aptitude and potential. Tracking via IQ or aptitude testing was a given. People understood some kids were smart and some weren't. Children who could do the work and didn't (there were no diagnoses of ADD or dyslexia or autism) were left back a grade. Parents were stoic, hoping that not being promoted, a family disgrace, would teach the kid a lesson. Lack of performance was not excused by emotional difficulties or social circumstances. You passed or you failed. Report card days were anticipated with great trepidation, even by "good" students. In addition to letter grades for academic achievement, students were also graded for deportment and cooperation, often called on the report card "self-control." Lack of ability in arithmetic was somewhat understood, but a bad grade in behavior was punishable. A child who did not suffer the consequences of a bad grade was dubbed "spoiled." There was no Ritalin for kids who didn't pay attention; there were consequences.

Rebecca Bass was my fifth grade teacher. I felt kindly towards her immediately because she shared my mother's first name. She was thin, dark and intense looking. I was told at some point that she had an ill husband at home confined to a wheel chair. Perhaps that accounted for the intensity. In addition to teaching fifth grade subjects, she was an artist, so our class time for art was particularly energetic and creative.

I liked to do art work. I doodled faces in all my notebooks and thought I had talent. I didn't. But she saw how much I loved drawing and painting and suggested I go to art school. The Fleisher Art Memorial Art School in South Philadelphia was free, but students had to get a recommendation from their school principal to be admitted. Mrs. Bass went to our school principal and obtained that permission for me. For a number of years, after fifth grade, I took the Seventh Street trolley car on Saturday mornings to my art classes, carrying a large cardboard easel under my arm, which opened to reveal the current class project. I also carried my chalks, paints and charcoals, whatever materials we were using that day. My hope was that the other passengers on the trolley car would understand that I was a child with a gift. It wasn't until many years later, when I acknowledged how untalented I was in art, that I understood Mrs. Bass' determination to boost my self-esteem.

Mr. Hyman, my sixth grade teacher, had his class produce a newspaper, and I was given the job of "class news editor." My excitement was indescribable. Each editor had a yellow cardboard sign, fashioned so that it stood upright on the desk, with his or her editorial designation printed in red letters. The sign was taken from its nest inside the desk and placed on the desktop whenever we had newspaper time in class. For me, this was utopia. I had known since second grade that I wanted to be a newspaper reporter, and here was my verification. We produced this newspaper several times throughout the duration of sixth grade.

One day I lost my sign. I was devastated, sure I would lose my job if Mr. Hyman did not see that sign on my desk. I tried to duplicate it by buying yellow construction paper and a red pencil. The reconstruction of the sign worked pretty well: I was able to make it stand up, but the red pencil I used was a little less vibrant in color than the one Mr. Hyman had used. I diligently printed "class news editor" on the sign, attempting to duplicate his printing as much as possible. Each time we had the newspaper class after that I was terrified that he would notice that my desk sign was not as accomplished as the others. If he did, he never mentioned it.

The elementary school that served our South Philadelphia neighborhood was "Fell School," named for a noted Philadelphian, David Newlin Fell. Everyone walked to school, even though there was a major street crossing to get there, Oregon Avenue. Traffic lights were at every corner and were diligently obeyed. Before the days of crossing guards, it is my recollection that a policeman was stationed at each corner before and after school hours to direct the children safely across the street. Those were the days when our parents told us to have reverence and respect for "the cops."

Because summer vacations held no special activities, no day camp, no overnight camp, no family trips, nothing but street playing, I was always ready and eager to start school in September. Most kids were bored with summer leisure by then and ready for a fresh school year with new teachers, whom we regarded with frightened respect, and the opportunity to buy new school supplies, which always meant a trip to our neighborhood corner candy store.

I went there often after school. The store carried more than candy and ice cream. I bought all my school supplies there, and the excitement of starting back to school in September was heightened by the importance of a visit to the school supplies section of the store. Construction paper was the essential purchase, promising hours of cutting and pasting for class projects. Along with that had to come a box of brass fastening clips with doughnut-shaped white cloth reinforcements. There were bright pencil boxes, with pictures on the covers and secret compartments. Each year I had to convince myself that even though these cost more than loose pencils, they included a pencil sharpener and a two-sided eraser, one for ink and the other for pencil, making this purchase a bargain. The crispness of virgin loose leaf pages, the sharp smell of the binder, the decision of choosing between a two-ring or a three-ring — these choices made this expedition a wonderland. A shelf in the back of the store housed an aging collection of "National Geographics." I headed for that shelf every time a new subject was introduced in history or geography. What wonders those pages held!

The first day of school in a new term meant wearing a special dress, but the next day regular school clothes went into effect. Although children's wardrobes were quite limited, they were divided: school clothes and dress clothes. Girls wore dresses, or skirts and sweaters as they approached teenage years, and dress up clothes were reserved for visits to relatives, holidays and family events. We often outgrew them before they became outmoded, or outworn. They then got passed on to another family member or a neighbor.

Our mostly immigrant parents had a reverence for teachers and education virtually unknown in today's in-your -face -world. They would no more have considered questioning a teacher's judgment, right to punish, or her authority, than they would have chosen to return to the world they left. Teachers were infallible, and we kids had better believe it. This regard was transmitted to the children, sometimes by mere osmosis; other times by greeting a complaint about a teacher, or homework, with the steely "the teacher is always right."

Not only did we accept teacher edicts, no matter how unfair we might think them, but our regard also meant we thought their lives were totally different from ours. Teachers were of another world; if one happened to mention a relative, a mother or a sister, we were awed. "She has a sister!" we uttered under our breath. Could it be she had a life similar to ours? To see a teacher outside the context of a classroom was astonishing: they went to restaurants, to the movies, they walked down the street. Incredible!

Each class housed about thirty students. We sat at old-fashioned school desks, the bench attached to the desk by ornate iron legs. The wooden desks often had carvings imbedded in their surface, sometimes a heart with two sets of initials. Set into the upper right was a glass inkwell and to its left a narrow depression for a pen. Despite chamois-like pen wipers, papers, books and clothes were often ink-splattered. The desktops opened to reveal a space for school supplies, books, homework, and non-school related paraphernalia accumulated over a term. Sometimes there was pilferage, and if the culprit went undetected, the entire class was punished. That usually meant staying after school, arms folded on the desk, in complete silence. On rare occasions a substitute teacher appeared, followed by the unwritten law of the class. Make her life miserable that day!

A cloak room was immediately adjacent to the entrance of the classroom. That was where we hung up our coats, jackets, or whatever outer wear was appropriate for the season. On rainy days, puddles framed each pair of galoshes, sitting on the floor under the transparent or slicker raincoats. On snow days, icicles surrounded the boots in the same way, and the steamy smell of wet fabric surrounded the cloak room and found its way into the classroom.

The blackboard was often covered with arithmetic problems or outlines of history time lines or whatever the current lesson was. Sometimes students were called upon to erase the chalked blackboards with an eraser which then had to be cleansed of the chalk residue by banging two erasers together, which usually meant a trip to the fire escape so the cleaning could take place out of doors. The impact of one eraser against another created a white wispy cloud accompanied by an unfamiliar faint odor. This chore was considered an honor, and if one child was called on to do this too frequently, he or she was immediately dubbed "teacher's pet," an insult tinged with envy.

The teacher sat at an imposing desk in the front of the room — no circles to equalize positions. Corkboard walls were often hung with students' outstanding work: art or compositions. I remember one classroom where the walls were lined with photos of classical musicians and composers. Beethoven's photo with his shock of dark hair dominated the lineup. The last one of the group was a completely bald Smetana, and I wondered if the composers had less hair as they approached our modern times. "Smetana" in Yiddish means "sour cream," and I always saw those words superimposed on the composer's name.

Once a term our elementary school had "Mothers' Day," when all the mothers were invited to sit in the back of the classroom to witness a lesson, and then, take the opportunity, in full view of the children but in whispered tones, to have an individual parent/teacher conference to ask "How is my child doing?" The question did not mean: how does he or she relate to others, nor did it mean how is his or her self-esteem? It meant: is my child smart? Are the grades and test scores good? Is my son/daughter obedient in class? Does he/she do the homework? Achievement was the name of the game. Only academic excellence could take these children of immigrants out of the cauldron of the American ghetto and justify the most courageous act their parents had ever committed: leaving what was familiar, no matter how unpleasant, for the unknown. No wonder they wanted their kids to be educated and become professionals. It was the step up that would make the difference for generations to come and justify their decision to leave their home, often leaving parents and siblings behind as well.

Thomas Junior High School was directly across the large concrete play area that separated it from Fell School, and in seventh grade, that's where all the elementary school children transferred. But the excitement accompanying that move across the concrete lake signified lots more than another grade. Junior High School meant being a teenager with all its attendant excitements and tribulations. This move also involved choosing a major, academic or commercial, which would affect our future career, friends, social and economic circles. We would also change classes, have different teachers for different subjects, get to know a cross-section of our grade, and meet classmates who came from other elementary schools. Many changes awaited us.

I chose Latin as my language. Dr. Miller was our teacher. I had never before had a teacher with a doctorate; probably didn't even know what that degree meant. She was in love with Latin and transferred her affection for that ancient language to me and many others in the class, except on a particularly obstreperous day when we brought her to tears with the frustration of keeping us quiet. Behind her back we chanted a litany in that class: "Latin's a dead language, as dead as it can be. First it killed the Romans, now it's killing me."

The physical education teacher had the job of teaching

"health;" a veiled synonym for a beginning sex education class where we pored over clinical pictures in a textbook of sperm meeting egg. The boys and girls were separated for "health education," which was just as well, as giggling and sideway glances took a lot of class time. Those teachers also had the unhappy task of teaching subjects such as personal hygiene, which doubled the amount of giggles and glances.

Boys and girls were also separated for more practical classes in shop and home economics. No one ever questioned these gender distinctions. Girls took sewing and cooking. Boys took shop and made wooden benches and tool kits. Girls in sewing class made white aprons to be worn in cooking class. Those who were skilled in sewing even made their white dresses for graduation. I bought mine and later attempted to dye it pink, with disastrous results. In the days before electric sewing machines we learned on treadle machines. I could never make my treadle go forward. I flunked sewing. In cooking class, we made dishes which never appeared on our kitchen tables at home: white sauce with peas is one I remember with particular distaste. Dishes we saw at home, such as brisket, kugel, tuna salad and Jell-O were not on our teacher's menus.

Part of our cooking class education was focused on how to wash dishes. Two dish pans were presented, one filled with detergent in which to dip the plates after they were scraped, the other with clear water for rinsing. The rinse water didn't remain clear very long. This process was new to me; I was accustomed to all the dishes being dumped in the sink, washed thoroughly with Rokeach kosher soap, put in a drainboard and then dried with a dish towel. I regarded the two dishpan idea as wholly American, and my first purchases after my marriage were two dishpans and a drainboard, gratefully substituting an automatic dishwasher when that became possible.

One of the highlights of Thomas Junior High was the after-school variety show which was held once every term. Admission was ten cents and every level of talent was seen. This was South Philadelphia in the '40s, and the future crop of famous talented pop singers lived there, many of them students at Thomas. Eddie Fisher was half a grade ahead of me and the auditorium seats were crowded with his fans, for the neighborhood already knew he would be famous, so we supported "one of our own." I didn't go to hear Eddie Fisher. A classmate of mine, George Shoester, had a wonderful voice with a style that imitated Frank Sinatra. That was worth my dime anytime. He went on to have a modest recording and performance success for a few years using the name "Georgie Shaw." We all know what happened to Eddie Fisher.

Tenth grade meant high school, and the junior high schools in South Philadelphia sent their students to South Philadelphia High School. There were two separate schools at Broad and Snyder, again separated across a concrete expanse, one school for boys and the other for girls. South Philadelphia High School for Girls (or Boys) was somewhat cumbersome, so the name of choice then, and still is "Southern," although today and for a long time these schools have been combined into one building with coed classes.

We came from the schools of our childhood, elementary schools and junior high schools. The schools of our neighborhood, where our friends went, where we played in the playgrounds, where we learned about doing homework, where we played tag and had relay races, schools with names like Taggart, and Key, and Fell, and Thomas, and Sharswood; Kirkbride and Furness and Baldwin and Wilson and Vare and Audenreid. This was our extended neighborhood and we were going to high school.

Our mothers and fathers were proud of us. Perhaps we were even the first of our family to go to high school, so many of our parents were immigrants, so many of them unschooled, but all of them knew that in America, education was our ticket to a career if we wanted it, possibly to a better marriage. Maybe we could be to our children what many of our parents could not be to us, because we would be educated.

It was a new experience to attend an all girls school. I liked it and am sympathetic to the old-fashioned yet increasing support for single sex education. We had the chance to bond into serious friendships with other young women without the presence and distractions of males around. We also had the opportunity to achieve without the inbred idea that boys were smarter and would get further.

Yet, there was also an unease about the separation. Just as boys were entering our lives we were going to segregate ourselves with other girls five days a week. But, in another way, it was freeing, a relief not to be on stage all the time, not to worry about what we said in front of them, or how our hair looked, or whether or not to wear lipstick. Some of us were allowed to wear lipstick to school; others, not until we were 16, like black dresses. Not until you're 16, our mothers said.

So we arrived at that imposing grey stone structure on an early fall day in September of 1944. World War11 was winding down, and by that time we knew we would be victorious. Shortly after we came to Southern, our president, Franklin D. Roosevelt, made a visit to the Navy Yard in South Philadelphia, and classes were dismissed so we could see him. We ran to the windows and to the sidewalks on Broad Street so we could catch a glimpse of this beloved president. And there he was, in an open car. No bubble, no protection. How naive we were then, and how safe he was. His ever-present cape flowed, the cigarette in a holder dangling from his smiling mouth, arms waving to us, the girls of Southern. Would we ever forget that day?!

And then he was gone — April 12, 1945, unable to share our country's joy on the day of victory. Germany was defeated, the European war was over, and a few months later, on a hot August day, we danced in the streets because Japan was also defeated and the world was free of tyrants, we thought then. And the boys came home. Our brothers, some of our fathers, and boyfriends. How dramatic it was to have a boyfriend in the military. Some of us wrote to cousins and pretended to our partners in study hall that they were boyfriends for the duration.

Our romantic fantasies were enhanced by song. The big bands were at the height of popularity. Didn't we sometimes cut school to go to the Earle Theatre to hear them? Woody Herman, Tommy Dorsey, Benny Goodman, Harry James, the music of our teen-age years, all the bands overshadowed by the one voice, the voice that sang to each of us individually. He means me, we knew those words were meant for us, and we could daydream about the crush of the moment as we listened, dreaming, eyes closed, to the voice of Frank Sinatra. Once or twice we even went to The Earle to see him — in person. We went early in the morning, and kept moving up for each show as the audience left.

So much entered our lives in those days. We grew up on movies, the glamor queens and handsome leading men of Hollywood shaping our vision of a life we never expected for ourselves, but we participated in that life as we sat in those hard seats at the Grand, the Colonial, the Ideal, the Jackson, the Broadway, the Savoy to see Betty Gable, Joan Crawford, Rosalind Russell, Clark Gable, Henry Fonda, Judy Garland, all those American names and American faces.

Was fashion an issue for us? Of course. Not only for prom gowns, but we dressed in uniforms. Not real ones, but sociologists would call them uniforms — skirts, mostly plaid, sweaters, mostly pastel, saddle shoes, mostly brown and white, and bobby socks. That's how we got the name which characterized our adoration of Sinatra. We were the generation of bobby soxers. A big fashion issue of the day: Should girls be allowed to wear pants to school? We called them "slacks" in those days. It seems such an old-fashioned word today.

High school was exhilarating for me. I liked my classes, I liked most of my teachers, I liked my friends. I felt almost grownup. Some of the teachers even called us "Miss" with our last name. I found most classes challenging and many teachers innovative. The school drew from a large geographical area which affected the diversity, creating a new and exciting mix of friends. During my time there, Southern for girls was chosen by the Board of Education for several experimental educational programs. We students didn't know it then, but our exposure was heightened and our intellect challenged. Possibly because of the Depression and unavailability of jobs, we had teachers who might ordinarily be teaching at university level. Our gain.

During lunch time we stuck our hands out of the openings in the iron fence that surrounded the school yard and exchanged pennies with vendors for salty soft pretzels and Italian water ice. When I see today's sterile pretzels emerging from electronic ovens I am reminded of the superior taste and texture of those soft pretzels from the dilapidated wooden cart.

The school also felt responsible for instilling some social values into its population. Our Eleventh Grade Tea meant wearing hosiery and heels, pouring from a silver tea service, and standing about chatting without giggles or screams. I suspect our faculty felt a responsibility to show us the possibilities of a social world less insulated than our own. Our social studies teacher spent a full class before the senior prom discussing prom etiquette and appropriate behavior. She told us not to order the least expensive item on the menu as that might embarrass our date, but to order the next least expensive item to make sure he could afford it. The school motto, "Noblesse Oblige," was a reminder that we had obligations to our community and was emphasized in every graduation speech by every class valedictorian.

We were to herald a generation we didn't recognize those days at Southern. Our futures were pretty clear to us in 1947. College for some, jobs for others. Jobs we could be proud of: bookkeeper, receptionist, maybe even private secretary. And for those who went to college, we anticipated careers, mostly as teachers. But always, marriage, children and family. Those traditions moved us to our expectations of what our lives would be. Marriage, children, a family. We'd make a home. We'd be the wife, the mother. Then came the '60s. By that time, some of us had children who were on the edge of the Flower Children generation. We worried about them, and were grateful if they were too young to participate in the youth culture. But there were other voices buzzing in our ears, voices that said this life is not enough for women. After the dinners are made and the laundry is done and the children are gone, what's left for you? We listened. Some of us went to school, many others went to work. And we learned the world is bigger than we thought, and we were glad to be part of a social world less inhibited than our own.

School meant public school. Private school was for rich kids and we didn't know any. For South Philadelphia Jewish families, Hebrew School equaled in importance our secular education.

We didn't go to Sunday School or religious school once or twice a week. Hebrew school was serious business: Monday, Tuesday, Wednesday and Thursday afternoon, after regular school, for two and one half hours, plus the same amount of time on Sunday mornings. If you subtract recess, assemblies, art, gym and music, the time spent in Hebrew School equaled our daily secular school time.

We had several subjects: Hebrew, of course, where we learned to read and write using the first five books of the Bible as our text. But this was before the establishment of the State of Israel when Hebrew was rarely used as a conversational language, so to this day I can read Hebrew, but my conversational skills are limited to about thirty unconnected words. Then there was literature, where we studied the literature of the Jews, concentrating on writers like

Sholom Aleichem and Peretz. History was as expected, a history of the Jewish people, from Biblical times through the Diaspora, up to what was the present for us. In the days before and during World War 11, we studied shtetl life and European migrations of the Jews. For those who went to Hebrew school after the war, studies must have had a very different focus. We had written tests and oral exams and homework. Probably our classes in Hebrew school plus our secular school education equaled what is taught in any Jewish day school, except we spent double the time in classrooms combining public school and Hebrew school.

I attended JEC2, which meant Jewish Educational Center #2, part of a network of independent schools called, usually, a "Talmud Torah" or referred to in Yiddish as "Cheder." This institution was not synagogue-affiliated but part of a central education system. Classes and offices were housed in a building at Marshall and Porter Streets, a typical school building with three floors and a wonderful auditorium. The building was a kind of art deco-style. Wide front steps led to a center hall and then to the large auditorium, where typical school-wide events were held: plays and holiday celebrations, religious observances and special events. Many years later, the building was utilized as a senior center operated by Philadelphia Jewish Community Centers.

Attendance at this Hebrew school almost mitigated the necessity of belonging to a synagogue. There was no need for additional opportunity for worship. We celebrated all holidays through the school, and the entire family was welcome to join any event. The children were involved in all aspects of presentation or observance.

When I was about eight, studying Bible stories, I asked my teacher a question: "Why," I said, "if God knows everything, did He permit Eve to eat the apple." A curious look passed over the teacher's face. "Ask your mother," was her answer. It took quite a few years for me to understand why she didn't want to deal with a reply.

We celebrated every holiday with a play to which parents and grandparents proudly lent their presence. In my first year of Hebrew school I was in a Chanukah play. Because so many of the parents, and all the grandparents, were immigrants whose English language skills were modest, plays were presented in English and Yiddish. My part was to run across the stage, stopping front and center, to announce in Yiddish, "Hannah is dead, Hannah has died, threw herself over the wharf and lies there with her seven children."

When I think back to my seven years of Hebrew School, I am full of wonder at the quality of the teachers. Mr. Blank taught Hebrew, a brilliant man who wrote fourteen novels in a language not yet used other than for worship. Mr. Sankowsky taught us history. I learned years later that he was an accomplished artist whose work was exhibited throughout the city. Dr. Levitsky, the principal, had a PhD, an impressive accomplishment in those days. His wife, a striking exotic-looking brunette, taught us music and directed our dramatic productions.

We had no confirmation, no bat-mitzvah. Those ceremonies were for more upscale neighborhoods. Our parents thought them frivolous; it was the learning that mattered. In our South Philadelphia culture, boys were bar-mitzvahed but girls were also educated in Hebrew school in coed classes.

My memory is that there were no bar-mitzvah classes for the boys, who had to study with a Rabbi or Melamed (teacher.) My brother was tutored by a special bar-mitzvah teacher who came to our house several days a week for a year. My father, who lost no opportunity to increase the educational opportunities of his children, had Mr. Shafritz stay a little longer each session to teach me to read and write Yiddish. So long as I knew the basic Hebrew alphabet (Yiddish uses the same alphabet but substitutes letter vowels for the symbols used as vowels in Hebrew) he argued, it would be a simple matter. It wasn't, yet I can still work my way around large print in a Yiddish newspaper. Book texts are somewhat harder and I give up easily.

Some families, eager to pass on their Socialist political leanings to their children, sent them to Jewish schools that de-emphasized the religious aspects of Judaism and focused on political and cultural issues. I met many graduates of these schools several years later when I joined the Zionist youth group.

Education extended beyond regular school and Hebrew school. No opportunity was overlooked and children may have balked but cooperated. Some families went beyond the conventional music lessons and, with fantasies of elegance and sophistication in their children's future added cultural pursuits. Dancing lessons had their rewards in recitals and drama classes in performance. Music lessons took precedence and diligent practice was rewarded by inclusion into the school orchestra. Violin lessons seemed prevalent with piano not far behind. I once expressed an interest in piano lessons, or perhaps it was expressed for me by my mother. She immediately contacted a local piano company, Wurlitzer, who offered a free piano with piano lessons at $1.00 a clip, and the piano stayed as long as the family endured the lessons. The pianos had seen better days; they were used, old uprights, but my parents were intrepid. The company brought the piano to the house, but it wouldn't fit into the doorway. Our house had limited living space behind the barber shop, so the piano had been destined for an upstairs bedroom. When it wouldn't fit through the doorway, the delivery men conceived the idea of tying a rope around this well-worn piano and hoisting it up to the second floor from the outside of the house. Fortunately that plan was abandoned and that was the end of my musical career. I suspect it's just as well.

As both art and music as potential life work had been forfeited as possibilities before I was ten, I had no regrets, for I knew from the time I was seven that I wanted to be a writer. I came home for lunch one day and told my mother I knew what I wanted to be when I grew up. "I want to be an author," I told her. My mother was an avid reader and perhaps I thought I knew that would please her.

"You want to write books," she stated.

"No," I said, I want to write newspaper stories." Retrospectively, I see that as an odd statement for a second grader who probably had not yet read a newspaper.

"That"s called a 'journalist'" my mother informed me.

"Okay," I said. I was very compliant.

"You'll have to go to college," responded my mother.

"Okay," I said again, without any knowledge of what that word meant, I'm sure.

From that moment on, my ambition never faltered.

It was not typical in the late forties and early fifties for the daughters of immigrant families to go on to college. In my high school graduation class of more than 300 women, less than a dozen went on to higher education. Those who did most often majored in education, as becoming a teacher seemed the route to go for many, with a profession that was respectable, whose vacation and holiday times coincided with children's school recesses, and could always be resumed when children were grown. A college education was often considered a stopgap measure for girls, until their real lives began with marriage. However, despite this conventional approach, parents were proud of their daughters who achieved a college degree.

On my graduation day from Temple University, my father closed the barber shop so he and my mother could attend the ceremony. A hand-lettered sign on the door informed the neighbors "Closed because of daughter's graduation from college." When they returned and reopened the shop, they brought out a bridge table covered with a white cloth. On it stood a bottle of whiskey, shot glasses, and slices of home-made cake so that the customers could share in their pride. Higher education was such a priority among immigrant families, when my friend Rita started as a freshman at the University of Pennsylvania, her mother accompanied her on public transportation for the first day of school to drop her off at the campus.

I recently went to my neighborhood dry cleaner to collect some clothes. The store was owned by a Korean couple. I found the door locked, with a hand-printed note which read: "Closed to attend daughter's graduation from college."

CHAPTER SEVEN
Getting Better

Most neighborhood doctors had offices in the front part of their houses with a side entrance to differentiate the office from the residence. Physicians were all male. Occasionally, we heard of a woman doctor, but I never knew one when I was a child. Usually the doctor was a young man whom the neighbors had watched grow up and cheered on through medical school, not an easy task for Jewish men in the days before World War 11 when entrance quotas to medical schools were well known and accepted. Their graduation was the pride of the neighborhood. Often, a parent's home was reconstituted so that the downstairs rooms became the doctor's offices and the family lived upstairs. Or, in the first neighborhood I remember, the parents moved to a corner home at Ninth and Ritner Streets so that their sons — both were physicians — could share the downstairs as offices.

These brothers, Harry and Lou Beloff, shared a waiting room, previously a family living room, with several examining rooms behind. No appointments were necessary; patients just walked down to the corner and took their turn. No receptionist, no nurse, no physicians' assistant came to usher in the next patient. You waited for your "next," just as you did at the grocery store or beauty shop, and then went in to see the doctor. Appointments were for specialists and that was a fear-filled anticipation. These consultations were rare and frightening, and boded serious problems. Before the days of medical insurance, doctor's visits were for real illness, not checkups. Routine medical care was not often an issue in the family budget so visits were saved for serious symptoms. A standard fee covered all office visits: 50 cents is my recollection.

These were the days when doctors made house calls. It was not at all unusual to see the doctor, between or after office hours, trudging up the front steps of one of our row homes, black bag in hand. A house call cost more than an office visit, probably $1.00, so these visits were limited to extreme illness. Privacy was not a consideration. Everyone knew when a house call was made and in rapid sequence the nature of the illness, the doctor's diagnosis and the prescribed treatment became everyone's business. As the doctor walked back down the steps, one of the family children could be seen scurrying to the corner drug store, prescription in hand. Medical secrets were nowhere to be found.

But even a visit to the doctor's office was a last resort. Home remedies were tried first, and each family seemed to have a "maven," an expert in the field of diagnosis and treatment. In my family it was "tante Rochel," an in-law relative but nevertheless an expert. Chest colds were her specialty and mustard plasters her mode of treatment. If I can reconstruct the procedure, a piece of coarse fabric, perhaps burlap, was coated with a wet pack whose main ingredient was mustard, not the wonderfully yellow kind that works so well with hot dogs, and not from the gourmet stoneware jars that come from France that we so like to number among our larder acquisitions. Perhaps it was just the simple mustard spice that sits on our spice shelves. It was mixed with warm water and some other variety of herbs and/or spices. This was placed across the back or front of the chest, depending on Rochel's determination of the origin of the ailment, and the coarse fabric, coated with the fast cooling yellow mud, burned and scratched intensely as it was applied. Sandpaper on fire is the best description I can give to how it felt. Protests in the form of screaming and squirming were greeted with "It's for your own good," a phrase that was to become part of the lexicon of childhood. This was soon followed by, "This will make you better," an explanation that was greeted with extreme skepticism.

If the home remedy didn't work another step was tried before a visit to the doctor's office. An interim interventionist was the neighborhood pharmacist. His medical expertise was considered only slightly secondary to the physician's and he was always available to answer questions about symptoms, patent medicines, and general health advice. His specialty was removing foreign objects from the eye. Mothers didn't attempt it because this was the province of the pharmacist. Can you imagine any pharmacist doing this in today's litigious society! But we didn't think any danger would result from this consultation, and it didn't. All foreign objects in the eye were shown to the pharmacist who left customers waiting while he performed this procedure. This was usually done with a Q tip, followed by a splash of sterile water. Back went the child to the playground in the street. The pharmacist always wore a white coat, which emphasized his medical authority to perform alchemy.

Corner drug stores always had giant glass urns of colored water in their windows. I don't know what they signified, probably just medicine. Outside the drug store was a lineup of telephone booths with doors that closed to ensure privacy, except from the adjoining booth.

But illnesses did get better. After the assault on the back or chest, a child could expect a hot drink of tea, honey, and perhaps a touch of Four Roses to aid sweating and sleeping. This delicious concoction was often accompanied by rock candy, crystallized sugar in irregular angularity, a string running through each piece, enabling the patient to swing and chew, swing and chew, or suck the sweetness after dipping the candy in the hot tea. Sweat was the panacea for all illness. For some reason ginger ale, too, seemed to have medicinal qualities. So when a bad cold struck, having survived the mustard plaster, it really wasn't too bad to spend a day home from school, in bed with a warm quilt, allowed to sleep late, library books and coloring books at hand, sometimes cutting paper dolls with changes of clothing, spread out on the quilt. The radio on the bedside table was always on so that all radio soaps could be heard, not only those available during lunch or after school, and we could reach out, whenever we wanted, for the hot tea, the sugar candy, or the fizzy ginger ale. Pineapple juice also had a place in this equation, so any dehydration that took place from the sweating was compensated for by the abundance of liquids by the bedside. The proverbial chicken soup was an added component to the getting better sources, although I suspect any hot liquid cascading down a sore throat felt good.

Home remedies often included the hated enema. Somehow a purging was considered the first step toward wellness, no matter the ailment. An alternate treatment was the vile-tasting castor oil, quickly followed by orange juice in an attempt to cover up the taste.

Feet were always an issue to be reckoned with and any childhood problem was solved with orthopedic shoes, usually unnecessary but part of parental doing the right thing. I wore ugly brown laced shoes until junior high school, when I assured my parents I would die if I didn't have brown and white saddle shoes. To add to the seriousness of the selection of orthopedic shoes, there was the foot x-ray machine so that the shoe salesman could more easily judge the degree of misshapen or misaligned feet. No concerns of excessive radiation existed.

Contagious diseases were another matter. I remember a print-ed yellow paper affixed to some front doors announcing that a contagious disease had invaded that household. Ailments such as diphtheria, scarlet fever and whooping cough came under the ju-risdiction of the city health department, which had the authority to affix those fearful yellow sheets to the front door. These were notices of quarantine, meaning enter at your own risk, and I sup-pose, people already living in the home should not leave for fear of infecting others. It was a great relief to the neighbors when the sign was removed, signifying the crisis was over and the house was no longer contagious.

A worse notice, though, was a purple sash hung on the door-way of a house, signifying a death in the family. This was not true of Jewish homes but was a fairly common practice among Christian families. This evoked hushed voices among the neighbors, appre-hension on the part of the children, but social graces came into play and the neighbors made appropriate condolence calls.

Language was engineered to limit the names of body parts and functions to acceptable synonyms. All anatomy below the waist was referred to by the generic "stomach." When my moth-er had a hysterectomy, I told relatives she had an operation on her stomach. As a teenager, the word "uterus" would never have crossed my lips in speaking to another person. Families often had their own private names for bodily functions and genitalia. A pregnant woman was referred to as "in the family way," and a man with a limp because of a prominent hernia was described as someone with "a bad leg." Urination was dubbed "passing water" and constipation or diarrhea as "stomach trouble."

My father, too, brought a degree of medical professionalism to the family. In old time Europe, barbers were also surgeons. (Hence the red, white and blue colors of the barber pole, sym-bolizing blood, bandages and veins.) In the Middle Ages, barbers performed surgery, bloodletting and tooth extractions, along with their tonsorial duties. Some of these medicinal features continued through the centuries, and although surgery was not among his skills, coupled with hair cutting and shaving, my father learned how to do "cupping," in Yiddish, "bonkas," a procedure akin to bloodletting. The implements consisted of small glass vials, wide in the middle and open at one end, a bit like miniature brandy snifters without the stem. They were a little larger than shot glasses and were used in the same way leeches were used: to draw bad blood to a spot that would cause an illness to improve. These never drew blood, but were applied to the skin hot. The cups were heated by a match and were then placed over the offending area. The flame removed all the oxygen from the cup, so that when it was placed open side down, a vacuum was created which affixed the cup to the skin, which was then drawn up into the cup. This was supposed to force the blood to the area and rid the body of the ailment. About a dozen cups might be used at a time, all applied to the area determined to be the hotbed of disease.

My father carried his cupping paraphernalia in a doctor's medical bag, which, when not in use, sat in the window of the barber shop with a hand-lettered sign: "We do cupping." I remember many nights, after the shop was closed and my father had eaten his dinner, when he took his doctor's bag and left the house to attend to his patient. I don't know what he charged, probably 50 cents, but I doubt it contributed much to our family income as most "patients" were family and good friends and he didn't feel it was proper to take money for health assistance. After my father's death I contributed his bonkas, complete with medical bag, to the Mutter Museum of the College of Physicians and Surgeons in Philadelphia.

A stay in the hospital was a frightening experience, as much for the family as the patient. Our neighborhood hospital was Mt. Sinai, at Fifth and Reed Streets, a hospital founded by the organized Jewish community to make certain Jewish physicians had a hospital in which to intern, take a residency and practice medicine because Jewish physicians were excluded from staff privileges in many hospitals.

My job as a messenger at the hospital lasted for summers until I was graduated from high school. My responsibilities were to check in visitors and bring new patients to their floors, including maternity patients who were about to deliver their babies, and I was to take them to the labor floor. In addition to introducing the patient, I was to tell the nurse, having asked the patient, if her water bag had broken. At 14, I had no idea what that meant, but I dutifully reported the information and wondered at the quizzical smile on the nurse's face.

I never knew about private rooms until I had that job. Anyone I ever knew who went to a hospital went to a ward, with anywhere from four to eight beds to a room. No one had medical insurance — I don't think it existed — and ward patients were generally considered "charity cases" and didn't have to pay. Even patients with private physicians spent hospital stays in a ward, visited by their physician who determined the treatment executed by nurses, interns and resident physicians.

Outpatient treatment for ongoing ailments was supervised at hospital clinics. With the advances of employee medical benefits, Medicare and Medicaid, and the social agencies that exist to attempt to ensure appropriate medical care, hospital clinics have largely disappeared. But in the '30s and '40s, these were a major source of medical care for South Philadelphians.

Hospital clinics were designated according to disease: the Diabetes Clinic, the High Blood Pressure Clinic, the Endocrine Clinic, etc. Being a clinic patient was a waiting game. Patients waited on long benches for their names to be called and the physician in charge could be anyone from the department chief doing his obligatory clinical work to a new intern learning the ropes. I remember taking days off from school periodically to accompany my grandmother to the Diabetes Clinic at the Einstein Medical Center, then known as the "Jewish Hospital," an institution also established to assure that Jewish doctors had a hospital affiliation. It was a long trip to that hospital. My Bubby and I took a trolley car to Broad and Snyder to board the Broad Street subway. We rode from the beginning of the line to the last stop, which was Olney Avenue and the location of the hospital. I accompanied my grandmother not only as her companion but as her translator. I was 9 years old. My Bubby told me her complaints in Yiddish, I translated them to the doctor in English, he gave me instructions for her in English, I relayed them to her in Yiddish. The process was time-consuming, but it worked. At times, an occasional doctor was fluent enough in Yiddish to conduct the conversation independently, but I was the language insurance.

The clinic route was the way many young children had their pediatric visits. Our neighborhood had a Well Baby Clinic, and that was where my brother and I received our shots and periodic examinations. But the school was a partner in the health care of children. At the beginning of every term, classes were lined up at the nurse's office, girls first, boys next. We were weighed and had an eye test. If the examination in the nurses' office determined glasses were needed, Philadelphia City Hall supplied them free of charge. For some reason, I wanted glasses desperately at about age 10. I cheated on the eye exam and was dutifully taken by my mother to City Hall to get glasses which I wore for about two days.

One of the more humiliating practices was the hunt for head lice. This was executed without any regard for children's feelings. Throughout elementary school, we kids were lined up in our classroom at the beginning of the term while the nurse came in and examined each head independently. We squirmed while she parted our hair, peered intently at our scalp, and sent us back to our seats, or, heaven forbid, to another, shorter line, whose mortified members took a note home saying this child has lice with instructions for eliminating them. My mother, convinced my frizzy curly hair was a welcome nest for those creatures, took matters into her own hands to make certain that note never came to her. Once a week my hair was scrubbed with brown soap, probably the kind that was used to clean floors. Then, my aching head was combed with a fine tooth comb until every hair squeaked with tension. Finally, portions were parted and my scalp rubbed with a burning liquid, which I think contained kerosene, as a final warning to those hateful creatures to stay away from this unwelcoming scalp! Just as my scalp stopped burning it was time for the treatment again.

Medical concerns and care meant overseeing physical complaints. I don't think I ever heard anyone, including my parents or parents of friends, worry about psychological trauma to their children. If children misbehaved they were "brats," or "bad," these adjectives used after a note from the teacher or a knock on the door from an angry neighbor. If kids were attacked by other children, they were told to fight back or take the medicine. Punishment was not meted out via "time out," but was often physical in nature. We didn't know the term "abused children" and would have been laughed out of the house if we threatened parents with reporting their treatment of us to authorities. Somehow we survived, even physical punishment, with the certain convictions of unconditional love and sacrifice on the part of our parents, despite angry threats and punishments.

I never knew anyone who consulted a therapist for children. None of the doctors we knew were psychiatrists. Only with education did we learn of the field of mental health and many of our generation became practitioners in that field. With knowledge came interpretation, perhaps excessive, of psychological damage and trauma that populated our emotional landscape during our childhood. As adults, many of our generation consulted therapists, pleased to have the vocabulary to describe the inadequacies of our upbringing and the lack of sensitivity in our relationships.

We were probably correct in our assessments, but I am convinced that the perpetrators of these injustices upon our psyches did the best they could, under the circumstances of their own pressured lives.

CHAPTER EIGHT
The Corner Candy Store

It was whispered in the neighborhood that he died of "dope." In the 1940s, that was a pretty mysterious word. The only thing I thought I knew about dope then was that musicians, especially drummers, used it because it helped them with the rhythm. Henry was no musician. Henry wasn't much of anything. I don't think he had a job, because whenever I saw him at Rosalie's Corner Candy Shoppe, he was sitting at the one round marble-topped table, on an ice cream chair, smoking cigarettes, which he bought one at a time for a penny each. He died at 41, and his chair stayed empty for a long time.

There were four chairs, and they were occupied every night. In my yet-to-come literary period, I would think of the evenings there as a "salon." The group gathered at 10 o'clock each night and sat around Rosalie's solitary table for about three hours. Topics of conversation could only be guessed. From random conversation in the neighborhood, I knew somebody's reputation

ACROSS FROM THE ALLEY

could be destroyed with half an evening's talk. Sex, politics, current events, and all kinds of intimate relationships were fodder for the agenda.

The four participants around the table did not include Rosalie. She sat on a high stool behind the counter, but she was the fulcrum of the group. One chair was occupied by Henry at night as well as during the day, and another by Dr. Gregory, the neighborhood doctor. He wasn't our family doctor; my mother said he had dirty fingernails, and anyway, she was a snob about osteopaths. Mrs. Pearlie Meyersman (everybody called her by her full name to differentiate between her and her ex-mother-in-law) was the third member of the group. She was divorced, a bleached blond, and childless, and she slept past 10 o'clock in the morning.

The fourth chair was occupied by my mother. Almost every night, after the dinner dishes were finished, with my brother and me in bed and my father asleep so he could get up early for work, my mother walked across the street to Rosalie's and stayed for hours. I often heard my father ask, "What do you talk about there all night?" "Nothing much," my mother would answer, with an offhand shrug.

Rosalie was the tallest woman I had ever seen. She must have been almost six feet tall and very thin. Her joints always seemed in conflict with the rest of her; they stuck out at angles from her body. She smiled a lot, but often her smile seemed rigid and fixed, without mobility, so that even when she said something serious or angry, the taut smile remained. Her attitude towards customers was equally chameleon-like. Sometimes she was friendly and helpful. One day I was sent to buy a bottle of ginger ale. When I left the store, I dropped the bottle on the sidewalk and watched, horrified, as the bubbles slithered toward the gutter. Rosalie, witness to my shame, gave me another bottle, free. At other times, she was curt and angry, chasing children and teenagers from the store when they lingered too long in front of the candy case or magazine rack. "This is not a hangout," she'd shout, her voice registering even higher than normal, overlaid with a thin gloss of despair that seemed to thread her speech, always. I expected a guttural sound to emerge from that lanky, long body, but her voice was clear and high-pitched, with a wavy undercurrent that suggested the possibility of hysterical outburst.

Rosalie never left her house. Her father, who also lived there, sometimes walked around the neighborhood. He was a gruff old man who never smiled, walked with his head averted and avoided saying "hello" to anybody. He always carried a cane with a shiny brass top but didn't use it to aid his gait; he just swung it in front of him. Even in warm weather, Mr. Steinbrunner wore a coat and a scarf. I never saw Rosalie clothed in anything but a cotton house dress, white apron and slippers, the apron strings wrapped several times around her matchstick frame. The after-school Rosalie, dispenser of bubble gum and ice cream cones, vendor of back-dated magazines and current newspapers, was hard to reconcile with the hostess of that intriguing midnight soiree.

Neighborhood matchmakers wondered if there might be some hope for an alliance between Henry and Rosalie. They seemed to be about the same age, and if the laughter and jokes wafting through the night air from the candy store were any indication of similar interests, they seemed compatible enough. Of course, there was always Mrs. Pearlie Meyersman, perhaps a rival for Henry's affections. Speculation ran high when Henry appeared once with an exotic brunette on his arm, but the two of them stayed in the candy store for only an hour. Henry left with her, to return alone later and take his usual place around the table. In the time he was gone, Rosalie led the laughter regarding the woman's too short, too tight dress, and the way her lipstick extended over her natural lip line. She was particularly venomous about the lady's breasts, which were apparently more than ample, and strained against a too small bra, stretching the sleazy fabric of an almost transparent rayon dress. I thought Mrs. Pearlie Myersman didn't have much to criticize about somebody' else's clothes. My mother told me: "You can learn from the bad habits other people have. Pearlie's clothes are always too short and the colors are too bright for a lady her age. When I asked my mother how old Pearlie was, she said, "That's a deep dark secret that only she knows." I was privy to the conversation between Mrs. Pearlie Meyersman and Rosalie about Henry's short lived girlfriend because it took place too early in the evening for the usual assembly, and my mother had sent me across the street to buy a milkshake.

Rosalie made exceptional milkshakes. They were thick and creamy and rife with ice cream. Sometimes my mother, brother and I shared one for dessert after dinner. I brought it home in the metal container in which it had been mixed, feeling the coldness penetrate my hands as I crossed the street. By the time I reached my front door, the outside of the cylinder was frosted and the tips of my fingers tingled. My mother washed the container carefully and then returned it to Rosalie, shiny and sparkling, when she settled there in the late hours of the night.

Sometimes stragglers stopped by on their way home from a late evening or to buy a newspaper or contribute some gossip to the group. But only Henry, Dr. Gregory, Mrs. Pearlie Meyersman and my mother were the regulars. And Rosalie. When Henry stopped in during the day, he and Rosalie were usually alone. Maybe that's why the neighbors speculated about a romance between them. But Dr. Gregory once whispered to my mother, "Forget it. Henry's not the marrying kind."

One day I heard my mother tell a friend, "Rosalie has the filthiest mouth I ever heard." That judgment had to spring from those conversations around the marble table. But I also knew that somehow her language and stories were more shameful because she wasn't married. My aunt, who didn't like Rosalie, complained about her to my father. "How does she know so much?" she asked.

When Henry died, suddenly and seemingly inexplicably, the matchmakers' thoughts turned to Rosalie. Her last chance had been buried, they said. Buried with Henry. I didn't notice any intense grieving on Rosalie's part; she didn't go to his funeral. Mrs. Pearlie Meyersman went with my mother. Dr. Gregory didn't go —too many patients in the hospital to see that day, he said. I heard my mother tell her sister that she thought Dr. Gregory might have given Henry too many prescriptions for dope and felt too guilty to go to the funeral. I decided Rosalie didn't go because her father wouldn't release her from working in the store. Although Rosalie seemed to be in charge, her father's ubiquitous presence always made me feel that he really ran things, and that Rosalie, grown up as she was, lived her life on his charity.

My mother's nightly appointment at Rosalie's was no secret. Her sister, my aunt Gracie, who lived around the corner, thought it a "disgrace" for a married woman with children to be away from her home so late at night, without her husband. When we first moved across the street from Rosalie's, my mother was campaigning for a Democratic candidate for mayor in a long-entrenched Republican city. The reason was three-quarters commitment and one-quarter payment. Her job was to knock on doors, distribute literature and convince voters it was time for a change. One night a few of the mayor's supporters, who dominated our ward, entered Rosalie's and blackened my mother's eyes, their way of saying "lay off." They knew where to find her, unprotected by her family.

My aunt was self-righteous after the beating. She told my mother it happened because she was where she shouldn't have been; where no respectable married woman would be at that hour of the night. My father was more philosophical. He said that politicians were dirt and if my mother didn't want to get beaten up again, she shouldn't work for politicians. My mother preferred my father's advice to my aunt's. She stopped her work for the Democrats but didn't give up the socializing at Rosalie's. That was my mother's introduction to and departure from ward politics. Rosalie was pragmatic about the episode. "Things like this don't happen to people who stay on the side of the winner," she told Henry the next day, who promptly reported this lack of loyalty to my mother.

Rosalie's older sister was also unmarried. Their living quarters, above and behind the store, were shared with their father, who crept around the store on stockinged feet, looking dour and grim. The neighbors felt sorry for these two old maids, poor things, stuck with this crazy old man. Emily was lucky, they said. She was a nurse who often slept at the hospital where she worked. At least she had a job and could get away from there. But Rosalie was like a prisoner, tied to the store and tied to the demands of her austere father.

Mrs. Steinbrunner, Emily and Rosalie's mother, had died just before I was old enough to cross the street by myself and go to the store at will, so I didn't remember her very well. My memory was of a gray-haired woman with glasses, as short and round as Rosalie was tall and thin. When she died, I heard my mother tell my aunt, "He killed her." I knew that couldn't be true because there were no police around. After Henry died and there was all that talk of dope, there was a resurrection of the gossip about Mrs. Steinbrunner. I heard some older girls, high school students, outside the store one day, giggling and whispering and comparing notes about the old man's trying to touch them. One of them, Doris, who already had a fur coat and was only 16, said that when Mrs. Steinbrunner died, she heard her mother tell her father that the old man had killed his wife because of his incessant sexual demands.

Rosalie watched us when a girlfriend and I came in to browse through the pile of backdated National Geographics, ostensibly for a homework assignment but hoping to catch sight of a brief loincloth or a bare-breasted woman in some foreign country. Her glacial laugh followed us out the swinging door. "Pretty soon you'll be coming in asking for the dirty best sellers in the lending library," she called after us.

As much as Rosalie smiled, old Mr. Steinbrunner was stern and gruff. He kept an old broom behind the counter and used it to chase kids he thought did too much looking and not enough buying. He was short and squat, with a huge turban of white wavy hair that made his head seem too large for his body. His lips were hidden under a sweeping walrus mustache, yellow with tobacco stains and drooping over his lips, so that the angry curses he hurled so often seemed to emerge from the mustache and not his mouth.

I marveled that Rosalie could be so nice to this crotchety old man. "Pop," she would say midafternoon, "Why don't you go up and take a nap? It's slow now. I'll take care of everything." Or, "Pop, it's so hot today. Why don't you go lie down in the back bedroom? There's a breeze coming in there now."

Sometimes, when I went to the back of the store to look at the new titles in the lending library and page through the National Geographics, I would find Mr. Steinbrunner sitting on a dilapidated old rocker, which creaked with every movement he made. Whenever the latest bundle of National Geographics was delivered, he was there first, avidly thumbing the pages. I sometimes saw him looking through magazines or leafing through the new arrivals for the lending library, sweat accumulating at the ends of the mustache, his fingers kneading the hem of his white apron, twin to Rosalie's.

In the winter, on a Friday or Saturday night, when I didn't have to wake up early for school the next day, I would take a long, hot bath, don flannel pajamas, get into bed and wait for the covers to spread their warmth over my body. Then I'd sit up, open the window a bit and feel the rush of cold air against my warm face, still flushed from my bath, and stare at the stream of light pouring from Rosalie's store. The voices attracted me the most. All was dark and quiet at that late hour, except for the light and the sounds that could be heard from within that place. In the summer, when doors and windows were open, the voices were clearer. Laughter and shouting could be heard for half a block, but most of the time there were just sounds, unintelligible no matter how hard I strained against my bedroom window, my face pressed against the tiny plaid of the mesh screen, struggling to hear what the grownups said.

One hot summer night I was awake long after my mother had left Rosalie's and was already in bed. The store was dark and the neighborhood was as still as it's possible to be on an oppressive night, heavy with heat. The only sounds were those night noises of coughing and flushing that penetrated the screened windows. My room faced Rosalie's bedroom with the span of a street between us. I thought I heard the soft sounds of a meowing cat, but as I listened, the sounds were clearly human. Plaintive, sad sounds, more a whimper than a cry. Then they got louder, and I heard Rosalie's unmistakable high voice, tinged with a terror that made me shiver in the heat. "Pop, please," I heard. "You promised never again, you promised to leave me alone. Pop, go away." The voice stopped, then turned into a long, low wail.

CHAPTER NINE

The Rite and Ritual Way

We bought spring clothes for Passover and fall clothes for Rosh Hashanah and Yom Kippur, the high holidays. The weather seemed always too cold for the new Passover clothes and too hot for the new fall clothes. It took a long time and a lot of explanation for me to understand that the dates of the holidays didn't change but the relationship between the Gregorian calendar and the Hebrew calendar did.

Holidays punctuated the sameness of days, the continuing emphasis on getting things done, going to school, shopping, playing; in general, our daily routine. Preparation for the holiday of Passover was frenzied.

I don't know how our grandmothers and mothers did it. No dishwashers, no prepared foods, certainly no outside help — and yet, somehow it got done. I hope it wasn't the holiday that contributed to a shortened life span for that generation of women. Yet, the expectation of repetition of the preparations, and the ceremony of the seder, were comforting in their continuity. Before so many contemporary creative Haggadahs with their inventive writings and improvisations were popular, we used the old Maxwell House Haggadah, a text familiar to me since early childhood. Maybe the company's distribution of these brand name Haggadahs was to give the subtle suggestion that Maxwell House coffee was kosher. When my grandfather was alive, my parents, little brother and I went to their house on Wharton Street for the ritual meal. I can still see my grandfather, imposing in a white kimono-like caftan, leaning on pillows as prescribed in the Haggadah, intoning the familiar story of the exodus. My brother was too young to participate in the ceremony, but I, a Hebrew school student, asked the centuries-old Four Questions.

We learned to say them in Hebrew School in two languages, Hebrew and Yiddish, and I dutifully asked them in both languages, intoning the singsong liturgy learned in Hebrew School. I remember being given sips of the sweet Passover wine, feeling indoctrinated in a world of grownups. I also felt very important, with all attention focused on me; also, nervous, fearful I would make a mistake. I didn't realize that family indulgence was part of the game and all would smile gently if I slipped up. Passover was celebrated for its full eight days with ritual foods. On the eighth day I was sent to the nearest bakery to buy the first bread. My mother always grumbled that the bakery opened too soon which elicited a discussion of whether the holiday was over before lunch or before dinner, an argument still unresolved. When we children came home for lunch in elementary school and junior high, Passover foods awaited us.

We all had two Seders on two successive nights and spent the next part of the holiday eating fried matzoh, gefilte fish and the special holiday dishes which, for some unexplained reason, certainly not sacred, we never prepared the rest of the year. Nuts were a part of the Passover table, walnuts and almonds and particularly filberts. These were the perfect shape for marbles, and we could be seen, in our new Passover clothes, kneeling on the sidewalk using those nuts for a game of marbles

The solemnity of Rosh Hashana and Yom Kippur were not lost on the children. Our Hebrew School classes prepared us for the synagogue observance, and activities at home prepared us for the family observance. When my grandfather was alive our family went to the Orthodox synagogue he and his "Landzleit" (fellow Zhitomirites) had founded soon after their arrival in their new world. I went with my father, a long walk from our home but travel by trolley car was prohibited, and I ran down the aisle of the noisy and busy synagogue to see my grandfather. I then left my father and grandfather and went to the balcony where the women did their praying and gossiping to see my grandmother and accept the admiration and blessings of her friends and family. In Orthodox synagogues, then and now, men and women are separated for worship. Today, it's often with a macrame or sculpted screen; the older synagogues had, and still have, an upper balcony for the women.

After my grandfather's death, we no longer went to the Orthodox synagogue but celebrated most holidays at my Hebrew school, where full services were held on these holy days. Once I was graduated from Hebrew School I joined my girlfriends to "hang out" at the neighborhood synagogue. Sometimes temporary romantic alliances could be forged on the steps of the synagogue. We probably spent more time on the outside than the inside of the building.

When the shofar blew to signal the end of Yom Kippur, great excitement pervaded the congregation. People greeted each other with warm embraces, smiles and good wishes for the coming year. Many family arguments were resolved as sisters and brothers greeted each other and agreed to hope for a better year among themselves. Children presented mothers with flowers and people went home to enjoy the meal after a 24 hour fast. Boys knew, once they were bar-mitzvahed, they took on ritual responsibilities. Girls probably felt they had more flexibility but most assumed 13 would work for them, too. This was before the days of the bat-mitzvah, at least in the provincial observances of South Philadelphia, and being graduated from Hebrew School involved a graduation ceremony but not a confirmation.

Chanukah was not nearly the celebration and anticipation it evokes today. It was never mentioned in public school, despite the fact that the population of my elementary and junior high school was predominantly Jewish. There was no expectation of equal coverage. Christmas was celebrated in the schools with a tree in every classroom and assemblies singing Christmas carols weeks before the holiday. An unwritten, unspoken agreement among the Jewish kids was that when we sang the carols, lustily and with pleasure, when the name of Jesus Christ was mentioned our lips were sealed. To my knowledge, no parent ever asked for this and no one discussed it; it just was. I don't remember feeling cheated or inferior. Christmas just didn't belong to me, and Chanukah was no substitute. There were no decorations and no expectations of eight gifts. Sometimes friends of my parents' or relatives gave Chanukah "gelt," a small offering of cash. A quarter was considered a windfall. We did buy chocolate coins but Chanukah was treated as a minor holiday, which it realistically is. As Christmas has become the shopping extravaganza it is today, so Chanukah celebrations have proliferated proportionally. I succumbed when my children were young and went into the one gift per night routine, which I still do with my grandchildren.

Purim was recognized by buying Hamentashen at the local bakery and, if possible, providing "shalach monas," gift baskets for the poor; at least, those poorer than we. At Hebrew School there was always a play featuring Purim's main characters: Queen Esther, Mordechai, King Ahasuerus, and of course, Haman the terrorist.

We told the story of Purim and rattled our groggers whenever his name was mentioned, to great clamor and satisfaction.

The holiday celebration I remember with the greatest awe was Simchat Torah, which means the joy of the Torah and commemorates the annual ritual of the completion and restart of the reading of the Torah. We children marched around the auditorium holding a small paper Israeli flag, long before the State of Israel was a reality, with an apple impaled on the wooden flag holder, and a lit candle atop the apple, somehow held steady in the apple core. No one seemed afraid of fire, and nothing ever happened to make the annual repetition questionable. No candle ever fell to the ground, no child got burned. No one warned us to be careful. We just were.

Children were not omitted from life cycle events: weddings, bar-mitvahs, organizational galas. Families were often insulted if the whole clan wasn't invited. Invitations to celebrations were scanned upon arrival, to make certain they read "and family." Bar Mitzvahs, weddings, graduations, and all such events, occurring throughout the web of extended families, were major happenings. The invitation list was the most important piece of paper in the household for months preceding the event. It got added to and subtracted from regularly, and both intended and unintended slights were rarely forgiven. Families pored over table placements, trying to remember who was friendly, who was not, and sometimes trying to create a romantic match. Children's tables always existed at these events, producing a steady stream of kids leaving their places to check on their parents, or report some insult or punch from some older child. Fathers waltzed around the floor with five year old daughters, the little girl beaming in her pink organdy dress, satin sash and Mary Jane shoes. These children's tables existed long after the children were past being little ones; my cousin and I remember being seated at a children's table when we were 20.

The women seemed older then. In my grandparents'

generation, by the time the women were forty, they appeared only in a black silk dress on special occasions, (the same dress) hauled out of moth balls twice a year. Shoes were often black-laced oxfords. The women sat together, side by side in gold-painted Thonet ice cream chairs that lined the walls of the banquet hall. Frequently, they danced together, and only got up to dance in nostalgic hora type dances when the band played familiar Jewish music. These traditional dances often got people out on the dance floor despite protests. A lively dance called a "Sher" could be likened to a square dance. It required eight people. Horas got almost everyone out on the dance floor.

To bring a date to a family event was a serious declaration. A lot had to do with the cost of the wedding or other event. The family did not, could not, afford the cost of an additional guest if the date were frivolous and not a potential "fiancé." Certain courtesies had to be observed. The mother of the young man or young woman who made the request for the adult child to bring a date telephoned the mother of the bride, bar-mitzvah boy, or groom. Then ensued a conversation about the seriousness of the relationship. If it were deemed by the party-giver that the relationship "had intentions," then the date merited another place at the table, and permission was granted. Of course, that meant that the date was under scrutiny by the entire assembly and evaluated by telephone the next day.

The first time I took my future husband to a Zitomirer annual banquet, I was more nervous than the day of my wedding. I knew he would be examined from head to toe, as I knew that some insensitive ladies would ask "when's the wedding," and that my mother's phone would ring incessantly the next day to question the seriousness of the date. Retrospectively, I realize he was braver than I.

Other affair "rituals" were standard. Invitations to the ceremony and a "reception" were not frowned upon. Some people, not family or close friends, left after the ceremony and returned for dancing, coffee and dessert, called by the caterer a "sweet table." When caterers became more worldly, the sweet table became a "Viennese Table," featuring exotic pastries and confections.

Often the reception invitees attended the wedding ceremony, sometimes accompanied by non-invitees. No one was offended. It was understood that every penny counted, and some people weren't close enough to warrant the complete event. Receptions also served as a means of meeting young people suitable to date. "Crashers" were not welcome, but came anyway. The crashers were always guys, usually good dancers, who had their Saturday and Sunday night social events pre-planned, with a responsive audience of the young women already at the event, anticipating one of the crashers might emerge as a potential boyfriend.

The rituals that surrounded death and mourning were inculcated in children even before they understood what was going on. Our generation understood cemeteries before we understood death. Trips to the cemetery for funerals, before the Jewish New Year, and on other occasions such as the deceased's birthday, Mother's Day, or whenever the spirit moved anyone, were total family affairs. Children were not excluded from funerals or the "shiva," the period of mourning in which the family stays at the residence and other family members and friends came to visit and bring gifts of sweets and food to usher in a new period of hope and a sweet future. Today, families and friends often acknowledge a death by making a charitable memorial contribution which serves family nutrition a lot better.

When the early burial society for the Zitomir group was formed, their first act was to locate appropriate cemetery locations. They found their burial sites in a rural area southwest of Philadelphia in an already established cemetery, " Mt. Lebanon." It remains so to this day. Many similar Jewish organizations did the same, so across the way from Mt. Lebanon is Mt. Jacob, and not far from there, Mt. Sharon. Why these flat lands were named after mountains remains a mystery to me.

Whether a lack of baby sitter mentality or the more psychological view that it was never too early to introduce the realities of life and death was the reason, children were not spared cemetery visits, whether to a funeral or on routine visiting days. Attendance at funerals was also a family affair. I remember my grandfather's funeral vividly. I was nine, and the rite of passage started at his home, casket on display in the living room, but not open — according to Jewish custom. This was considered an appropriate setting for an observant but not devout man. My grandparents' store and house was at a corner, alongside a small street. My father's numerous cousins were in attendance, along with their children, several of whom were boys about my age. At nine, I was still oblivious to appropriate behavior at a solemn event, and my cousins and I played in the street until my mother, appalled at this lack of decorum, made short shrift of our playfulness on this sad occasion. When the ritual services were over and it was time to leave for the cemetery, the cortege wound its endless way to the site, at that time probably a two hour trip. I went along, as did my four year old brother.

Today, with grave-side services the norm, eliminating the drive from funeral home to cemetery, and with family members scissoring traditional shiva time because they live in other parts of the country, we don't often see the kind of funeral and mourning periods I experienced as a child. The way we acknowledge the death of a loved one has undergone changes, perhaps more civilized, perhaps more assimilated. While attendance of young children at funerals may have seemed bewildering and probably frightening to them, they understood, at an early age, the encompassing grief that this loss produced. Usually, the bereaved sat in the front row at the funeral parlor facing the closed coffin, accepting the often tearful condolences of relatives and friends who approached them in a long line. Accompanying my parents at funeral homes on this ritual down that long aisle always made me marvel at their seemingly effortless and uncanny aptitude to say the right thing under the circumstances. I was certain this verbal expertise was a talent that came with age, and I kept waiting for the time when the appropriate sympathetic words would come easily to me, equating this acquired skill with whistling and tying shoelaces successfully. Now, when I think I might be able to handle this funereal skill, I rarely am put to the test.

The family no longer follows the coffin out to the lobby of the funeral home in an effort to mask the public face of mourning, as the on-lookers are quietly dismissed row by row and hurried from the premises to their cars. Burial is often private, and ceremonies which took place at a funeral home have often been replaced with a memorial service, whose theme is usually to "celebrate" the life of the deceased rather than mourn his or her death. Today, it is not as common as it was for attendees at a funeral to have the opportunity to see the family before the services to express condolences. Often, the family is sequestered in a private room and escorted into the chapel just before the services begin, having undergone whatever private rituals are done by the rabbi before their public appearance.

The funeral I remember best was my maternal grandmother's. By then I was a teenager and funerals were old hat to me. I also had learned how to behave with the solemnity I truly felt. My mother and her two sisters traveled from the funeral home to the cemetery in the first limousine that followed the hearse. My cousin and I were in the limo with them, on the jump seats, and they had given the "honor" of traveling with them to Jake, the widower husband of my grandfather's cousin Rochel. The mood in the limo was somber; these three sisters were burying their remaining parent and not yet ready to discuss who had come to the funeral and who had stayed away, when suddenly Jake sighed, and said "Aistes Surah's geshtorben." (So, it's really true, Sarah has died.)

And so it went, on that interminable ride to Mt. Sharon where my grandmother was to be buried, about every 10 minutes, the long sigh, followed by the identical phrase: "Aistes Surah's geshtorben." After about the fifth exclamation, the three mourning sisters looked at each other askance. Laughter was certainly inappropriate considering the situation, but the temptation was irresistible. My cousin and I had no restraints: we looked away from Jake and tried to swallow our giggles.

The ride to the cemetery was just a prelude to what followed the shiva. It is traditional to leave the house of mourning through one door and return through another, signifying the initial mourning period is over and a new beginning is in order. There is precedent for this custom that originated with the synagogues of old. Upon the death of an important member of the community, the houses of study were shut down during the morning period. When the mourners returned to the synagogue, they were not to sit in their usual places but move four cubits from their regular position. We can see how that translated into leaving the house via one exit and returning through another door.

When the three sisters left through the back door of the shiva house to return via the front door, the family dog, housed in the back yard, decided this was an opportune time to go for an outing. He followed the women as they wound their way around the block to return to the house, prancing and barking behind them. They were overcome with laughter, but embarrassed to laugh on this customary mourning walk, so they leaned into each other to hide their natural reaction. The neighbors were filled with pity: here it was long days after the funeral and the daughters were still so overcome with grief they could not walk a straight line.

On the opposite end of the ceremonial spectrum, weddings were the acme of family participation. They were joy-filled events with beaming parents, enthusiastic support and a bride and groom who, although the stars of the show, had nothing to say about the process. Parental authority was dominant and months of planning, sending invitations, choosing an orchestra, huddling with the caterer, accompanied by sleepless nights of decision making, preceded the big event.

On the Sabbath morning before a wedding, the bridegroom to be was called to the Torah in the local synagogue. The women in the balcony then threw bags of candy at him, calling for a sweet future for him and his bride. I remember staying up late the night before my cousin's "uff ruff," (calling up) at my aunt's house, filling small white bags with mixed hard candy. I've seen this custom revived at bar and bat mitzvahs in recent years, and the scene at my aunt's house always returns vividly, as it did when my children were small and I filled Halloween bags with loose candy, not worrying about razor blades in apples or poisoned chocolate.

My parents were married at Stanton Hall at 7th and Synder. My father often told the story of their wedding preparations. My grandfather, as the butcher, prepared hundreds of chickens the night before. This was prohibition time, so the liquor — I suspect nothing but bottles of Four Roses — was laid in the bottom of a wagon to hide them and covered with the chickens. My grandfather steered the horse and wagon through the streets of South Philadelphia in the middle of the night to deliver the cooked chickens and the forbidden whiskey to the banquet hall. Where the rest of the food came from I do not know. Were the chickens refrigerated? Probably not. My family heirloom photos show a young pretty bride surrounded by yards of diaphanous veiling, flanked by a cherubic looking groom, in front of a backdrop of elaborate draping and flowers supplied by Slutsky's Photo Studio, nearby on Snyder Avenue. I never heard any stories of any guest suffering from food poisoning from these unrefrigerated chickens. Perhaps they were transported raw and cooked at the banquet hall. Perhaps they were packed in ice. I like to think precautions were taken.

Many of the affairs for the Jewish community of Philadelphia, particularly for residents of South Philadelphia, were held in the upstairs banquet hall of Uhr's Kosher Restaurant, euphemistically referred to as a "ballroom." I remember Uhr's particularly, the site of my brother's bar-mitzvah and my wedding, the guests assembled in a rectangular room, devoid of decoration, walls lined with gilt ice cream chairs. The only nod to convention was a raised dais for the band. The chupah (canopy) appeared magically for all weddings, and I imagine the photograph of the same chupah is standard in many a photo album of any wedding ceremony conducted between 1930 and 1960 at Uhr's banquet hall.

The attraction of this particular venue was that guests could assemble in the upstairs hall where the ceremony took place without passing through the street level dining room where ordinary diners were no doubt being hurried through their meal to make certain the room was empty and tables newly set for the wedding guests. At the end of the ceremony, guests were notified through a drum roll to descend the narrow staircase to the restaurant proper. When guests were seated at their tables, another drum roll announced the bride and groom entering the dining room, while the emcee/band conductor, announced "Ladies and Gentlemen, may I present Mr. and Mrs. _____! who descended decorously through the narrow doorway into the dining room to hearty applause from the guests.

The children's tables outshone all others, with their party dresses and suits. The little girls wore dresses with wide sashes and matching ribbons in their hair, which became undone by the time the ceremony was over, and the special occasion black patent leather Mary Jane shoes. The boys wore knickers until their bar-mitzvah when long pants made their appearance. They also wore jackets, which made it a quasi-suit, and abbreviated ties. By the end of the first course, the ties were askew, the shirt was hanging out of the pants, and their hair had lost its slicked-down splendor.

Fortunately, there were no psychologists in the family in those days to solemnly interpret the boisterous behavior of 27 three -to-eight-year olds, vying in a screaming contest. Fortunately or not, none of the parents knew about hyperkinectic syndrome, so any child whose behavior became really outrageous was treated to a slap in a strategic spot and threatened with expulsion from all future parties — until the next one.

Air conditioning was non-existent except for movie theaters, so from April until October windows were wide open, sometimes screened, sometimes not, on the second floor of the banquet hall. Through the long windows that fronted the street, with its narrow, confined store fronts boasting lingerie, linens, hardware items, and a plethora of household goods and clothing, the rumble of the street could be heard at intervals, adding to the lively music of the band and the reflection of the neon sign that announced the presence of the restaurant to any passerby.

The band usually consisted of three pieces: a piano, drums and a horn. The band leader often played one of the instruments, as well as acting as emcee, and sometimes he was the band singer. At a more extravagant event, a fourth musician might be added who played a bass fiddle or another stringed instrument, and a singer, usually a voluptuous red-haired female. The band leader, in his role as emcee, performed essential accompaniments to the activities: read congratulatory telegrams, acknowledged concurrent birthdays and anniversaries of guests, and generally kept things lively. That wasn't usually necessary; friends and relatives were there to have a good time. Their lives offered little amusement except for these special and welcome celebrations.

There was no doubt about when the evening ended. At a pre-arranged time between the hosts and the band leader, the band played "Good Night Sweetheart," and people took their leave, with many compliments to the parents of the bride and groom or the parents of the bar-mitzvah boy. We had no car. My father did not own an automobile until I was married. We went home late, on the trolley car, we children asleep in our parents' arms. The children were exhausted and sleepy, and were carried by their fathers to the corner trolley stop. Each awoke the next morning in his or her own bed, to ask in wonder, "How did I get here?"

CHAPTER TEN

It's All Relatives

Aunt Tillie lived around the corner, the mother-in-law in a second floor apartment over the corner grocery store and the sister next door. It was not unusual for all members of an extended family to live within shouting distance of each other, as they often did, over the porches and across the street. My mother's mother, her sisters and their families lived within four city blocks for all my growing-up years. Relationships were very different because of this proximity. All were involved in the raising of everyone's children. Advantages were a sense of family, a bonding of relatives, protection from what might be "bad influences," and a general sense of belonging. Disadvantages were everybody was in each other's face, and the neighbors were privy to family arguments, disagreements, and secrets which somehow leaked. Marital stress and children's disappointing report cards were fodder for aunts' and grandmothers' intervention.

Families seemed more connected in those days, not always

positively, but somehow always present. Parents seemed to know the friends of their children in a more intimate way than future generations. Even the transition from child to teenager seemed less traumatic in the '40s. Perhaps life in general was simpler, or, perhaps, just less complicated and adventurous than it is for teens today. We seemed to make the transition with minimal family angst. Parents didn't seem to worry as much about the self-esteem of their children, or how discipline should affect them. They did not question their authority or wisdom in directing children's lives, even teenagers. When there were conflicts with parents, we aired grievances in girlfriend intimacies.

Changes came slowly; a major leap for girls concerned cosmetics. We experimented. How could we resist the lure of lipstick and eye shadow. Popular magazines, that is, consumer publications for women and fan magazines, featured come-on ads that sent, for a mere dime, makeup samples. I don't think they came in plain brown paper wrappings, but a portion of my allowance made it to those companies quite frequently.

Future hopes for the children of these South Philadelphia families were ambitious but realistic, expressed not only by parents but by all the family as well. For boys, if they were smart and worked hard, a professional life of a doctor, lawyer, dentist, accountant, was hoped for. For less talented boys, a respectable business, more white collar than retail, was the ambition.

Sadly, daughters were not usually expected to pursue a professional career or higher education. Of course, there were exceptions, but a responsible office job after high school graduation, as secretary or bookkeeper, with the expectation of decent moral values and, with good luck, a respectable marriage and family, and the female child was turned over to her husband.

My extended family dynamic was probably not too different from most. The proximity of houses, the inter-relationships of friends and neighbors, and the perplexing ongoing narrative of family togetherness and family separateness affected the children's lives, because they were privy to arguments, reconciliations, and the undercurrents that compose family relations. Children, not sheltered from family problems and included in celebrations and life-cycle events, learned quickly how to establish an individual place for themselves within that extended family structure. I made independent, solitary visits to family homes, not realizing that there were times when I was an intruder; other times, a welcome guest. One night, bored with nothing to do, I decided to visit my aunt's house several blocks away. It was dark and rainy, which probably gave me a sense of adventure. I had been playing some pretend game wearing an old dress of my mother's and a discarded pair of high heels, and decided to show my aunt my invented costume. The weather didn't deter me.

Off I went in the dark and the rain, my destination about three or four blocks and several major streets away. But the amount of traffic in those days was limited and not so hazardous, and I had no restrictions about crossing streets, so off I went. Those children who did have restrictions about crossing streets would wait for an adult, and then say "cross me," and were always accommodated.

I seemed to be the only child out on this nasty night, but my determination urged me on. I arrived at my aunt's house, my "costume" dripping rain, slipping and sliding in my mother's shoes, now sloshy and wet. I walked up the steps to the house and peered into the small, lighted foyer and up the steps to the second floor. There, in the middle of the stairs, sat my cousin. Her long, dark curls had been freshly brushed and coiffed and cascaded like lustrous sausages over her shoulders. She wore a pink, fluffy robe, wrapped around her like a protective placenta, with matching pink slippers. I rang the doorbell, but immediately realized I would not be greeted enthusiastically and would probably be reprimanded by my aunt. I turned and ran down the steps, sliding in the shoes, and escaped down the street, unwilling to take the risk.

It's hard to know whether the frequent interaction with extended family members was due to real affection or merely proximity. Probably a combination of both, and this extended to in-laws. Marriage often meant another set of parents for the bride and groom, and more family members for the parents. The Yiddish word that expresses the relationship between children's in-laws is "machatunim." There is no corresponding word in English.

Although immigrant families reveled in the freedom they knew was part of their American life, there was still a wariness about government; sometimes even a fear of government interference; even "big brother." Because these people were all legitimate imports, they weren't concerned about deportation, except perhaps for political affiliations, but they knew they wanted no trouble from authorities. My father-in-law took it one step further. He didn't believe in getting on lists. He lived in the U.S. from the time of his emigration from Russia in 1908 until his death in 1958, and at no time did he become a citizen. It wasn't political philosophy that prevented his citizenship, but rather his general laissez-faire attitude about commitment. "Now, they don't know I'm here," he would say, "but once I become a citizen, I'll be on everybody's list." So for his half century tenure in this country he never voted, almost never filed an income tax return, and never registered for a pressing license which was required for all tailor shops in the city of Philadelphia.

I suspect that had he ever bothered to file an income tax form, the government would have come back and told him his meager income qualified him for welfare aid. He was not so much interested in avoiding taxation as in evading recognition.

In the six years of our joint occupancy of a house, every January when signs went up asking aliens to register, I trembled with anxiety that a black Mariah would pull up at our door in the middle of the night to collect him. Occasionally, I tentatively suggested to him that alien registration would not require him to become a citizen, but merely meant that the government would know he lived in this country. He looked at me as if I were totally mad, unable to understand his simple response. "That's what I mean," he said, "Why do they have to know I'm here?"

However, as he approached the age of 65 and noticed many of his fellow senior citizens collecting their social security checks, his manner became a little anxious. Was there something he was entitled to that he wasn't getting? My husband patiently explained to him that in order to be eligible to collect social security, one has to have, at some point, made some contribution to the fund. When he realized that meant filing an income tax form, he was crushed. After much agonizing and rumination, Dad made the decision: He would do it! He would do his share for Social Security!

Unfortunately for the accounting profession, few tax forms are as uncomplicated as my father-in-law's was to complete. My husband did it for him for several years, and, as usual, his income warranted no taxes, which we had been telling him for many years.

Finally, the first check from Social Security arrived, not for the $30 each month he was to receive subsequently, but with a retroactive payment of $400. This was a windfall. He was exuberant. I suppose he had some remorse about his list phobia in the past.

Some women, many years before "The Feminine Mystique," probably felt a degree of frustration in their daily lives, which were for many humdrum and confining. Organization affiliation often alleviated this, as well as volunteer work in institutions

Although volunteerism was not as much of an issue as it is today, or perhaps there were more pertinent issues in our South Philadelphia community, many of the women did try to incorporate charity work somehow in their lives. At Ninth and Shunk Streets was an orphan home for Jewish children, and people brought clothes and gifts when they could. My father went there one Monday a month when his shop was closed to cut the children's hair. It wasn't until long after he was gone that I learned that he did not charge the Home for the haircuts. It was pro bono work for him.

One block away, on Eighth street just above Shunk, was an old age home, called in Yiddish by everyone in the neighborhood a "Moshev Z'Kayneem," a phrase taken from the Hebrew and literally meaning "home for the elderly." My mother did volunteer work there, office responsibilities primarily, and was there quite often, never returning without sad stories of neglectful children or sick old folks. The frequent, and often expressed fear of our elder population was that they would wind up in a Moshev Z'Kayneem. This was a pervasive horror that persisted in people's minds. Would their children be unwilling to provide for them so they could avoid institutionalization? These were the days when there was no extra money to be put away for the proverbial rainy day. The expectation was that a surviving parent, or couple, would need to depend on their children and there was no shame attached. Rather, a smug, self-confidence assumed that they would be cared for, perhaps an unconscious or unspoken refund for their own caring investment in past years.

Many years ago, my husband and I picked up the mother of good friends to take to another city where her granddaughter was to be married. She was living at the Philadelphia Geriatric Center, a model at that time for this type of housing. When I walked into the lobby to locate her, I saw a prosthetic leg leaning against a chair, and the smell of urine was overwhelming. Then, I understood completely why my parents' generation shuddered at the possibility of this as their future. This is what my mother must have seen at the old age home on Eighth Street. These institutions were a far cry from the sanitized day care centers for seniors, or airy, well-staffed assisted care facilities we see today and which are so popular. Yet, I never pass one without thinking it's just a 21st century version of an old-fashioned Moshev Z'Kayneem.

Inhabitants of these institutions seemed much older then

than people of the same vintage seem today. I feel as if many of them would have been my present day contemporaries. I think of my grandparents, younger when they died than I am as I write this, and to me they were always old. Perhaps that's true of children of all ages.

All of the old cliches about grandparents turn out to be true. There is a special relationship that exudes total acceptance, no criticism or rejoinders — an all-loving exchange that never changes.

Saturday was the day I visited my grandparents. I awoke every Saturday morning with delighted anticipation, for my grandparents adored me. As the firstborn of their only beloved son I was special and spoiled by them. Nothing I could ever do or say could possibly disappoint them.

They owned a small Kosher butcher store near Fifth and Wharton Streets in South Philadelphia. This meant I had to take a trolley car to their house, about three miles from where I lived. The store was, of course, closed on the Sabbath and my bubby and zayde always planned a quiet day. That was easy to do. They owned no car, so visiting was restricted to relatives who lived within walking distance, for they would not use public transportation on the Sabbath. However, in the selective morality so common to grandparents, they never restricted my use of the Seventh Street trolley car on my Saturday visits.

These trips started when I was six or seven. My mother gave me a note which I handed to the trolley car conductor indicating my "stop." It stated: "Please leave my daughter off at Wharton Street." The motorman's sole responsibility was to operate the car and it was the conductor, housed in a cubicle up to his waist halfway down the center of the vehicle, who collected the fares, answered questions and settled the fights among kids who traveled alone, and observed, with a sharp eye, those street smart youngsters who tried to shimmy under the rail to avoid paying the fare.

I was much too virtuous a child to attempt that and solemnly approached the conductor with a token in one hand and my note clutched in the other.

No matter how frequently I made this trip, and I made it weekly for about three years, I always had concerns about the conductor's memory, so I sat directly at his elbow, and, five minutes into the ride, I set my eyes upon his face and never shifted my gaze for fear he would forget about me and my destination. I worried endlessly that he might ignore me and then what would I do? The world beyond Wharton Street was alien territory.

When I reached my stop, recognizing it myself but always needing the reassurance from the conductor that I was not mistaken, my grandfather was waiting for me at the trolley stop. My heart jumped at the sight of his familiar tall but stooped frame, for I knew he had remembered that I was arriving for our day together. There was always that fear, in the mind of a seven-year-old, that he might be too busy to remember.

During the two block escorted walk to my grandparents' house, I held my grandfather's hand, glowing with anticipation of their absorbed attention in me as we approached the butcher shop. In those days, when shop owners' stores were just an extension of their living quarters, visitors never used the residence door to enter the home, if indeed one existed. The door which led to the store was the one all guests, family members as well as customers, used. My grandfather and I would enter the store, which, on Saturdays, was bright and shining, having been scrubbed clean at closing time the day before. There were no meats or fowl in the showcases. The butcher blocks were spotless, perforated with thousands of gouges from the many slashes of the frequently honed knives which smacked the thick slab of scarred tan wood, relentlessly stabbing through the beef, liver, chickens, ducks, and entrails as customers awaited the raw material for their dinner. The odor of Clorox rose from the freshly washed floor, wafting up through the sawdust which covered it.

I was always drawn to the huge wooden refrigerator in the back of the store. It was a size unlike anything I had ever seen. The polished metal handles, attached to the broad wooden front of the doors, were resistant to the tug of a small child. I pulled hard until the door opened and then I would stand there, chilled as the cold air that arose from the refrigerator washed over me, mesmerized by the slabs of meat hanging on hooks: plucked chickens hanging by their necks; wet, shiny globs of liver, and the huge shoulders of cows suspended from the treacherous looking hooks. Organs on shelves, slick entrails and hearts and chicken feet with toenails still attached. The murky darkness and pungent smells of that re-frigerator frightened me but my habit was that I had to stare at its contents before I could begin my visit.

My grandmother had lunch waiting for me, and as there was no cooking allowed on Saturday, lunch consisted of the remnants of Friday night's dinner. My grandmother first offered me a cold jellied soup she called by its Russian name "P'tcha" and I've since learned from restaurant menus that it is the delicacy "calves' foot jelly." I rejected it then and still do, and my grandmother's offer-ing was a joke between us. She didn't know then that it was a high-priced item on French restaurant menus, starting with the word "aspic." To her, it was merely leftover soup that had jelled in the refrigerator overnight.

Their unstinting love for my father embraced me and my brother as well. But I was the firstborn grandchild and enjoyed the selfish privilege of five years of additional attention from them. When I walked into that purified butcher store on Saturday afternoons, holding my grandfather's hand, with my frizzy hair, brown orthopedic oxfords and cotton print dress, size "chubby," my grandmother's eyes lit up as if the Messiah had walked into her kitchen unannounced. Ten years later I was to see that same look on her face as she lay stricken in a nursing home, paralyzed by strokes and unable to speak. But when I arrived for a visit at the nursing home, as I did every Saturday afternoon, somewhat resentfully stealing the hour from my teenage life, and walked into the room to see her lying helplessly in bed, that same expression of complete acceptance of me crossed her face and helped me understand the mystique of unselfish and committed love. That future picture was nowhere in my mind on those earlier Saturday afternoon visits.

After lunch it was entertainment time. My grandparents had an ancient Victrola and had somehow acquired one American record in English: Dorothy Lamour singing a song from "Road to Morocco" with Bing Crosby and Bob Hope. The song was "Moonlight Becomes You," and my contribution was to sing along with the record and dance for them. I draped an old piano shawl across my shoulders as I pranced around the room, out of tune vocally and out of step with the rhythm. Their smiles made me feel like the most graceful and talented child in the neighborhood.

When the show was over, it was my turn to be entertained. I always went to a movie at a movie theater at Fourth and Reed, around the corner from my grandparents' home. In those days, no child ever cared what was on the screen (it was usually a puritanical Hollywood love story) nor did parents censor. The subject of the film was unimportant, as were the reviews, or even if it had been previously seen. It was on the screen; therefore, I went. My grandfather marched me around the corner, paid the eleven cents admission, and bought me a soft pretzel which cost a penny. When the movie was over, no matter the time, my grandfather was waiting for me. I sometimes wondered if he didn't just stand outside the theater and wait until the movie was over because he never failed to be there on time. It must have seemed to my grandparents as if days had elapsed because they never failed to suggest that I had stayed for two showings. I denied it vehemently, although I suspect there were times when I did.

It was often getting dark by then. My grandfather and I walked back to the butcher shop, through the store and into the room beyond which served as living room, dining room and kitchen. Dinner and my grandmother were waiting.

After dinner, the real purpose of my visit began. Before the popularity of health clubs and spas, sweating, swimming, and feminist consciousness-raising groups, I experienced all of these at the tail end of my day at my grandparents' home. My introduction was a neighborhood public bath house whose clients were the Jewish immigrant women whose families had settled in South Philadelphia. The place was known as "the shvitz" (Yiddish for "sweat"), and an evening spent at this working class imitation of today's spa was comparable to dining out and theater entertainment for that tired, over-worked community of women. The baths constituted the Jewish equivalent of a Kiwanis convention, the Union League clubhouse, a beauty salon and an elite getaway spa, all under one roof.

From early childhood, I was my grandmother's frequent companion there. The weary women who spent every Saturday night rejuvenating themselves at the shvitz spoke only in Yiddish, often unaware that I understood them. Retail stores or services were often open on the Sabbath, a concession to the commercial style of their new world. Although English was the language of my home, Yiddish somehow imprinted on me, and from my earliest speech, I was able to communicate with my grandparents in that colloquial and picturesque tongue. Unlike the standard "my parents spoke Yiddish when they didn't want us kids to understand them," I did understand them so there weren't too many family secrets I didn't know.

Although I was always the only child at the baths, it didn't seem to bother my bubby. I suppose it didn't bother me either. I was too young to understand that my presence at this adult women's night was exceptional, and I didn't mind being admired, pinched and smiled at by all the ladies. I knew I had been invited into a world that was not meant for me, not yet, and that pleased me. Probably my grandmother wanted to show me off to family and friends, and because they had no idea I understood their conversation, I was privy to all kinds of gossip, family secrets, and shared female confidences that might never have come my way had the women known that I understood them. In this way I learned of Aunt Tillie's change of life pregnancy, Mrs. Weiss' liver ailment, Dr. Fine's second wife, and about all kinds of gynecological complaints I didn't understand, and which remained mysterious to me for many years.

Many of the women who were part of this Saturday night at the shvitz were extended family. Cousin Rose, who learned from years of experience and cut fingers to be the manicurist in her husband's beauty salon somehow found relaxation in doing the same, without charge, for her sisters-in-law and cousins at the shvitz. Cousin Eta, a diminutive redhead with a fiery personality, who came late to the baths because she worked behind the deli counter in the small grocery store she and her husband ran in West Philadelphia, had a loud and hearty laugh, startling coming from this 4'11" possibly 100 pound energetic bombshell. Leaving the corned beef sandwiches for the trolley car rides that took her to the shvitz wasn't easy but evidently worth it. Everyone waited for her raucous laughter as she shared her week's encounters, always with a lewd undertone.

And cousin Esther, of the same diminutive proportions as Eta, who had spent the day shampooing customers' hair in her husband's salon, still had the energy to give pedicures to her relatives in the entrance hall of the shvitz.

The experience at the bathhouse always held great mystery in my child's mind. Some years away from adolescence myself, I was intrigued by the femaleness of the carelessly draped bodies, the loving care of the long, often graying hair, the sighs of relaxation, the unaccustomed self-indulgence, all hinted at inscrutable puzzles I could not understand. But I was not upset by my lack of understanding; I knew these were matters for grownups and my time would come. It was enough to have been invited into this sacred, secret world of women.

Most of the women seemed to be middle-aged or older — almost a tacit agreement that unmarried women or newlyweds were not ready for this experience. Somehow I was exempt, too innocent to understand the whispered confidences and adult laughter. They were right.

The building which housed the bathhouse was old and shabby on the outside, with faded paint and crumbling bricks, but the interior sparkled with white tile and shiny chrome, the air redolent with the purifying aromas of soap, antiseptics and cheap but powerful perfume. As a teenager, before I understood the value of sisterhood, I would recall these conversations as ordinary "woman talk." But as a child, this talk intrigued me. I barely understood the references to husbands and children, daughters-in-law and mothers-in-law, finances and bargains, recipes and illness, pregnancies and miscarriages, and the veiled sexual references that always drew a giggle or a nod. Somehow I knew I was privy to information that ordinarily would have been shielded from my young ears.

Each time I was at the baths, I invented an excuse to leave for a few moments, drawn to the stairs that led down to a darkened swimming pool in the building's basement. The water was still, serene and unrippled. I sat on the steps, halfway down, afraid to go directly to the water (I couldn't swim.) Anyway, it was dark, and all the childhood fears of darkness and the unknown accompanied my curiosity. Why didn't the women swim there, I wondered. It seemed a perfect cap to the intense bathing that was going on just a staircase away. Only years later did I solve the mystery of those enigmatic depths with the realization that I had been attracted to the "mikveh," the ritual bath. I never saw anyone in it; never even saw it lit. Sometime in the future I learned that there were special, reserved times for this immersion, and that certain rituals accompanied its use. Saturday night at the shvitz was not one of those times.

The gatherings at the shvitz were no models for feminist consciousness-raising sessions. These were women who spent a good deal of their time tired. Cousin Minnie worked behind the counter of a retail store as seller/cashier/guarantor of merchandise in a Mom and Pop business. Cousin Rose was the manicurist and color processor in her husband's beauty shop, as well as the mother of four children under ten. Cousin Eta sliced corned beef and salami behind the counter of her husband's deli. However, they were still wives and mothers, first and foremost wives and mothers, so that their responsibilities were heightened rather than lessened by their dual roles. But they never questioned dual career marriage, and certainly had no expectation of shared domestic responsibilities just because they shared business responsibilities. It just wasn't a time when women questioned their roles.

But it was a time when conveniences at home were minimal. Laundry was washed by hand in heavy metal tubs or in the bathtub with the help of a wood-framed, metal corrugated scrubbing board. Families on their way up boasted a wringer washing machine. Prepared foods were a generation away and dinner guests were frequent, which meant daily shopping partnered with inadequate refrigeration and storage facilities. A new arrival from back home, a relative who hit hard times, a friend passing through to see what opportunities were like, could always be certain of a meal, a pillow, and a place at the table.

Most of these women had been left behind when their husbands made the unknown journey to America to seek their fortunes. The women took care of children, parents, in-laws, and assorted relatives in what was to become a matriarchal society for a time, while husbands sought their future in the land of milk and honey, dealt with their disillusionment, sent money back to Eastern European countries to keep the family going in their absence, and then, finally, after reconciling the differences between their expectations and the reality, sent the necessary information for travel documents as well as passage money.

My grandmother was among that group. She had been left behind with two small children to await her husband's "success" and summons. The summons came six years later, and when my grandfather finally picked her up at the dock in New York, he discovered a diminished family. Their daughter had died of an undisclosed ailment a few months before my grandmother and her younger child, my father, were to leave. She decided to spare her husband this tragic news until their arrival, so he learned this when he greeted his wife and son after a six year separation.

These issues of past lives were seldom the topic of conversation at the shvitz. The present and future plans were more relevant. By Saturday night the tired women were ready for some relaxation. It was a time for pampering, a rare and unexpected treat. The entrance hall, in addition to the manicuring facility, acted as gathering place and social hall.

The oversized shower and bathing rooms gleamed with white tile, gracing both walls and floors, and randomly placed wooden benches were plentiful. Drains were positioned along the floor so that when showers and faucets were open the water ran in rivulets over the tile, negotiating its way to the nearest concave drain. There were no shower or bath enclosures. The shvitz was no place for modesty.

The sound of the ubiquitous running water, the smell of perfumed soap and shampoo mingled with lotions, all created a feeling of unfamiliar self-indulgence. A massage corner baffled me — why would people permit someone to pummel them mercilessly? Another thing that puzzled me was the steam room, although

I always felt compelled to thrust my face into that hot, humid cauldron for a moment and emerged gasping and ruddy from the steaminess that enveloped me. I never understood how my grandmother and her friends could sit there for twenty or thirty minutes at a time, absorbing the intensity of the heat, continuing to laugh and talk and take pleasure in each other's company in the midst of that boiler room.

When the women left the steam room they stood under a cold shower to soak themselves and feel refreshed — the total experience a forerunner of today's popular sauna. There were large wooden buckets placed around the room. My grandmother and I would drag one of them to "our bench" and after she washed my knotted hair with rancid-smelling brown soap, she filled one of the buckets with hot water and poured it over my head for a rinsing. As the soapy water cascaded into my eyes and nose, over my body and into the drain at my feet, no one could have been cleaner than she and I after those hours of soaking, sudsing and rinsing.

The bathing part completed, we were ready for phase two. We covered ourselves with white coarse dressing gowns, scratchy against my softened skin, and I can still feel the shock of cold air as we exited through the swinging doors of the bathing room to walk upstairs to the resting room. Now that I recall this scene through the layered backdrop of other experiences, it was more like a hospital recovery room. We were all exhausted and purified.

This room sported rows of cots with mattresses — no sheets, no bedding, just mattresses. Behind each cot was a metal locker which held clothing and other belongings. All the women lay down on the mattress ticking (no pillow) and settled themselves for a rest, but first, each would reach into a brown paper bag and pull out an orange to restore the body after the fatigue of the bathing. Somehow oranges were endowed with magical recuperative powers, and were supposed to replenish the body of whatever nutrients and strength had been washed away with the soap and water. As the oranges were peeled and eaten, I lay on my bare mattress and listened to my grandmother and the other women recapture their week and share plans for the future. These women must have known something about the restorative power of citrus. Many years later, I recalled this ritual as I watched my daughter's basketball team devour orange slices between game halves.

Adjacent to the central gathering hall/pedicure salon was a small tea room furnished with linoleum-topped tables and wooden stools. When the women felt sufficiently rested, they dressed, and before leaving for home, reluctant to relinquish their closeness and the difference from their daily lives, they lingered in the tea room where each had a glass of tea and some home baked cookies. Although there was a serving area that seemed capable of providing meals, I never saw anything eaten other than tea and cookies. The women drank the tea Russian style, in a glass swallowed through a sugar cube held in the teeth. I have never recaptured that melting taste of poppy seed-filled cookies crunching in my mouth, washed down by overly sugared tea as the women sat and talked, replenished and renewed by their bathing and conversation.

After our snack my grandmother began her protracted goodbyes and with many pats on the head and blessings for me from her friends, we began our trek back to her house in the dark night. The stars never seemed so bright, the streets so quiet, the bond so strong between us as we walked home from the shvitz, quietly holding hands.

CHAPTER NINE
Epilogue

Then it was over. I finished college, was married, and moved to another part of the city. Eventually, I followed the exodus of my generation and took my family to the suburbs. South Philadelphia, too, saw many changes in its demographics. The first wave of immigrants grew old, and, as their children left the neighborhood, they took various routes. Some stayed rooted in their old homes or moved to apartments and swayed with the changing tides of the neighborhood. Others, as they aged, moved to senior residences or nursing homes, depending on their state of health. Some moved with their children to other neighborhoods and took part in the growth of their extended families.

Today, the neighborhood looks much as it did in my years there. It does not look decayed or unkempt, but it still looks poor. Many of the corner stores have bowed to the influx of malls and have shuttered their plate glass windows and become part of the residence they once fronted. Seventh Street is still a business district but ethnic names from countries other than Eastern Europe spread across awnings and glass windows, and the contents of the stores reflect that ethnicity.

But the streets still belong to the children. Balls hurtle across the narrow lanes, accompanied by shouts of "you lose." The schools I attended are still there, with teachers perhaps involved with more problem solving than the multiplication table, a reflection of our cultural and sociological changes.

A tapestry crosses my mind, brocaded with the imprint of softer days and louder voices, the rich fabric woven through with the excitement of emotions on the surface, less contained and more high-spirited than our more civilized controls of today. Those who lived in that world live different lives today. The alleys are gone from their lives and the pool rooms are sophisticated billiard parlors. But the memories are embedded and will remain, sometimes wistfully, sometimes with no regrets at their passing, but they are always present.

The revival of memory, abetted by the waitresses' remarks, was soon enhanced when I attended a high school reunion, and the memories continued to rush into each other. As I drove through the familiar streets, I looked at the houses; the area still didn't look like a ghetto slum to me. It looked like a poor but respectable neighborhood. It wasn't until I took sociology courses in college that I discovered I had grown up in a ghetto slum. The neighborhood fit the description in the books: ethnically cohesive, poverty, houses in need of repair. I didn't even realize I was underprivileged or deprived.

There were times when my children were young and knew no other life than single suburban homes and local manicured parks, and I felt nostalgic for the easy-going, random, unsupervised play on the streets of South Philly. One day I thought I could share my memories with my children and I took them on a subway ride and walked them through my old neighborhood.

"Why are the houses stuck together?" they wanted to know, and "Where's the garage?"

Perhaps Thomas Wolfe was right. Perhaps you can't go home again.

Time often sweetens memories. The sense of a vibrant, involved community heightens. Each adult who grew up in South Philadelphia has a story to tell. This was mine.

Breinigsville, PA USA
06 April 2011
259237BV00003B/5/P